Conversations with Gordon Lish

Literary Conversations Series
Monika Gehlawat
General Editor

Conversations with Gordon Lish

Edited by David Winters and Jason Lucarelli

University Press of Mississippi / Jackson

www.upress.state.ms.us

The University Press of Mississippi is a member of the Association of American University Presses.

Copyright © 2018 by University Press of Mississippi
All rights reserved

First printing 2018

∞

Library of Congress Cataloging-in-Publication Data

Names: Lish, Gordon, interviewee. | Winters, David, 1983– editor. | Lucarelli, Jason, editor.
Title: Conversations with Gordon Lish/ edited by David Winters and Jason Lucarelli.
Description: Jackson: University Press of Mississippi, 2018. | Series: Literary conversations series | Includes bibliographical references and index. |
Identifiers: LCCN 2017057788 (print) | LCCN 2018000919 (ebook) | ISBN 9781496816269 (epub single) | ISBN 9781496816276 (epub institutional) | ISBN 9781496816283 (pdf single) | ISBN 9781496816290 (pdf institutional) | ISBN 9781496816252 (cloth: alk. paper) | ISBN 9781496818164 (pbk.)
Subjects: LCSH: Lish, Gordon—Interviews. | Authors, American—20th century—Interviews.
Classification: LCC PS3562.I74 (ebook) | LCC PS3562.I74 Z46 2018 (print) | DDC 813/.54 [B]—dc23
LC record available at https://lccn.loc.gov/2017057788

British Library Cataloging-in-Publication Data available

Books by Gordon Lish

English Grammar. Palo Alto: Behavioral Research Laboratories, 1964.
The Gabbernot. Palo Alto: Behavioral Research Laboratories, 1965.
Why Work. Palo Alto: Behavioural Research Laboratories, 1966.
A Man's Work. New York: McGraw-Hill, 1967.
New Sounds in American Fiction. Palo Alto: Cummings Publishing Company, 1969.
The Secret Life of Our Times: *New Fiction from Esquire.* New York: Doubleday, 1973.
All Our Secrets Are the Same: New Fiction from Esquire. New York: Norton, 1976.
Dear Mr. Capote. New York: Holt, 1983.
What I Know So Far. New York: Holt, 1983.
Peru. New York: E.P. Dutton, 1986.
Mourner at the Door. New York: Penguin, 1986.
Extravaganza. New York: Putnam, 1989.
My Romance. New York: Norton, 1991.
Zimzum. New York: Pantheon, 1993.
Epigraph. New York: Four Walls Eight Windows, 1996.
The Selected Stories of Gordon Lish. Toronto: Somerville House, 1996.
Self-Imitation of Myself. New York: Four Walls Eight Windows, 1997.
Arcade. New York: Four Walls Eight Windows, 1998.
Krupp's Lulu. New York: Four Walls Eight Windows, 2000.
Collected Fictions. New York: OR Books, 2010.
Goings: In Thirteen Sittings. New York: OR Books, 2014.
Cess: A Spokening. New York: OR Books, 2015.
White Plains. Stroud, UK: Little Island Press, 2017.

Contents

Introduction   ix

Chronology   xv

Gordon Lish Interviews Gordon Lish   3
   Gordon Lish / 1965

Gordon Lish   11
   Amy Penn / 1988

Captain Fiction: Super-Teacher Gordon Lish   17
   Gail Caldwell / 1988

Captain Fiction Rides Again:
The Further Adventures of Gordon Lish   22
   Lisa Grunwald / 1989

Feeling Uniformly Jewish: An Interview with Gordon Lish   27
   Mario Materassi / 1990

Interview with Gordon Lish   35
   Patricia Lear / 1990

Gordon Lish   43
   Alexander Neubauer / 1994

Gordon Lish   60
   Douglas Glover / 1995

A Conversation with Gordon Lish   67
   Rob Trucks / 1996

Self-Interview   96
   Gordon Lish / 1996

An Interview with Gordon Lish   101
   Deron Bauman / 1996

Molly Bloome Talks with Gordon Lish   107
   Molly Bloome / 2002

Interview with Gordon Lish   126
   John Lee and Vernon Chatman / 2009

Gordon Lish, The Art of Editing No. 2   137
   Christian Lorentzen / 2015

An Interview with Gordon Lish   153
   David Winters / 2015

Index   167

Introduction

The writer, teacher and editor Gordon Lish is among the most influential figures in modern American fiction. Spanning over half a century, Lish's career has encompassed the counterculture of the 1960s, the rise and decline of so-called literary "minimalism" in the 1970s and 1980s, dramatic transformations in book and magazine publishing, and the rapid growth of creative writing instruction, characterized by Mark McGurl as "the most important event in post-war American literary history."[1] Today Lish is known primarily for his radical, and controversial, editing of Raymond Carver, an intervention that proved decisive for Carver's writing and reputation. Nevertheless, Lish's impact reaches far beyond Carver. Over the decades, he has discovered, published, promoted and mentored two generations of major American writers. As an editor at *Genesis West* (1962–1965), *Esquire* (1969–1977), Alfred A. Knopf (1977–1995), and *The Quarterly* (1987–1995), and as a teacher both inside and outside the university system, Lish has worked closely with many of the most inventive writers of recent times, including, for instance, Ken Kesey, Neal Cassady, Grace Paley, James Purdy, Jack Gilbert, Stanley Elkin, Harold Brodkey, Cynthia Ozick, Barry Hannah, Joy Williams, Amy Hempel, Mary Robison, Lily Tuck, Anne Carson, Will Eno, Sam Lipsyte, Diane Williams, and Ben Marcus. Alongside teaching and editing, Lish has also written over a dozen books of his own. Praised as "reminiscent of Stein or Beckett," his complex and comic avant-garde prose commands a loyal readership.[2] But despite his role as "one of the major formulators of the canon of contemporary American fiction," Lish has been neglected by literary scholarship.[3] Partly because of the outcry surrounding his rewriting of Carver, as well as the sensationalized coverage of his "cult-like" writing classes, Lish has become, in the words of his friend Don DeLillo, "famous for all the wrong reasons."[4] In this collection of interviews, we hope to highlight some of the right ones.

Published in a variety of venues, these interviews cover Lish's entire career in literary publishing, from his early years in the Californian little-magazine scene of the 1960s, to his tenure at Knopf in the 1980s, when he occupied what *Esquire* called "the red-hot center of the literary universe."⁵ But they also chart his departure from that center, after his editorial career ended. Lish's professional trajectory illustrates what McGurl has called the "inside-outside" dialectic of post-1960s literary culture: an "institutionalization of anti-institutionality" whereby being "way out" became, for some of the period's key players, a route in.⁶ In the 1960s, Lish's countercultural credentials helped win him his editorship at *Esquire*, where his unconventional tastes (and maverick "Captain Fiction" persona) later attracted the attention of Knopf. There, as he recalls in conversation with Douglas Glover, he found himself "remarkably free" to pursue a distinctly uncommercial agenda. Publishing was changing, however, and Lish's freedom couldn't last forever. By 1994, a wave of corporate consolidation had drastically altered the industry, and even Knopf—an imprint traditionally driven by prestige over profit—could no longer accommodate his loss-making list.⁷ Over the course of these interviews, then, we witness Lish moving from the outside, to the inside, and back out again. In the late 1980s, Lish's interviewers encounter him at the height of his powers, firmly ensconced in the Random House offices. Thirty years later, Lish has become a living reminder of a bygone age: "a country no longer extant," where "the publishing fiefdoms of Manhattan were proud castles in the sky," where "editors were princes and writers kings."⁸

Even during his time at the center, Lish was unruly, rebellious, combative: a true outsider-insider. Several of these pieces see him espouse an "outlaw principle," which he relates, variously, to the "difference" and "apartness" of Jewish identity, to literary-critical models of the agonistic and antinomian (from Harold Bloom to Leslie Fiedler) and to his defining obsession: revision. Revision, for Lish, is more than a means of editing manuscripts; it is a full-fledged artistic credo. Interviewed by Mario Materassi, he quotes Franz Kafka: "the positive is already given, and it remains to us to accomplish the negative."⁹ Revision is the key to this process: a "reversal" and "overturning" of anything fixed, anything "normative." This principle permeates Lish's theory of writing. In conversation with David Winters, he outlines one of his trademark techniques, the "swerve," an idea borrowed from Bloom, and now employed by hundreds of his former students. With every consecutive sentence, Lish claims, the writer must "say no to what is prior," continually "controverting" previous assertions, and thereby performing "a refusal rather than an approval." Like his early role model, Ralph Waldo Emerson, Lish associates creative practice with perpetual self-revision, and with the evasion of any position that ossifies into orthodox routine. This commitment is richly affirmed throughout his interviews. Lish's ideas are always "evolving," to quote his interview with Amy Penn—transforming, maintaining their "rate of growth." Being an artist, he tells Alex Neubauer, means staying one step ahead of the game: as soon as one finds oneself classified or institutionalized, one must "move on to a new space."

The most important of these conversations date from a period when Lish himself had moved to a new space. In 1986 he taught the last of his university-based writing classes, turning instead to private instruction. Over the next decade, Lish's private classes fostered a flourishing of innovative fiction—something akin to a new avant-garde—that persists to this day. Lish's private teaching was, in his words, "the purest thing I do," and its purity depended on its distance from mainstream writing instruction. By the 1990s, America's burgeoning MFA industry had already drawn scathing critiques; for John Aldridge and others, writing programs were factories for formulaic "assembly-line fiction."[10] Aware of this risk, Lish sought to give students "that which was available nowhere else." As he explains to the *Paris Review*, his teaching consisted not of a "workshop" but a "performance," an improvised discourse with no fixed format. In keeping with his revisionary outlook, he meant for his teaching to be irreproducible, insusceptible to standardization. As Patricia Lear notes, "Lish the teacher is not made for the textbook but rather for experience." Usefully though, Lish's interview with Alex Neubauer provides an accessible overview of the techniques he taught in class. This conversation will prove invaluable for literary critics—and, more importantly, writers themselves—intrigued by the mysteries of Lish's teaching.

"I'm a dynamic conversationalist," Lish half-jokes in the first of these pieces, one of two in which, with typical playfulness, he interviews himself. Yet even when conducted by someone else, an interview with Lish is Lish's show. One would expect nothing less from an author whose novels and stories are narrated by, variously, "Gordon Lishnofski," "Gordon (Gordon!)" and "Gordon. G-o-r-d-o-n. But call me Gordo" (as he once wrote to DeLillo, "Lish's books star Lish. Kisses, Lish").[11] In the fullest interview he has yet given about his fiction, Lish tells Rob Trucks that the "monologue" is his "only form." Similarly, his spoken responses often unfold into intricate monologues, improvised on the spot, while somehow still staying (and here we have the essence of Lish) entirely within his control. In this respect, Lish's interviews are of a piece with his writing and teaching: all three are strands of a single performance. Lish's extraordinary verbal performances have been the medium for his influence, and for his fashioning of that mythological figure we know as "Gordon Lish." But they also contain a practical lesson. In the classroom, his students recall, the point was to pay attention "not just to *what* Lish was saying, but *how* he said it"—how he swerved from one place to the next, spontaneously, but with utmost precision.[12] Along the way, he creatively combined, and revised, the raw materials of his life—the exploits, encounters and relationships which have made him such a central presence in modern American letters. Lish's spoken style was partly inspired by his early friend Neal Cassady, whom he recalls could "conduct with me a conversation of impeccable flare, *whilst* recapitulating for me the five other conversations audible in the same room, *whilst commenting on* those five simultaneous recapitulations."[13] The same is true of the conversations in this collection, which interweave a lifetime's worth of literary activity. In so doing, they also convey the very core of Lish's teaching: the imperative to keep moving and changing. As Ken Kesey once said of Cassady, of Lish we might say: "the virtue of continual, engaged experience—an endless and relentless argument with the self—that was his lesson."[14]

✦ ✦ ✦

This project was conceived in the summer of 2015, during an extended research trip to Gordon Lish's archive at the University of Indiana, Bloomington. Each evening, we checked in with Gordon by phone or email about the day's discoveries, and about the objects of his obsession at the time, some "terrific fried chicken wings" he had once enjoyed in a supermarket on College Mall, and which he urged us, with characteristic fervor, to find. Over the weeks, those wings took on a fantastical aspect, coming to seem as significant as the rest of our work. Regretfully, we never found them, but our broader research was more than rewarded. History will recognize Lish's vast contribution to literary culture; in the meantime, we hope that this book will whet people's appetites. In addition to individual copyright holders, we wish to thank Ethan Lish, Jonnie Greene, and, above all, Captain Fiction himself, for everything.

DW
JL

Notes

1 Mark McGurl, *The Program Era: Postwar Fiction and the Rise of Creative Writing* (Cambridge MA: Harvard University Press, 2009), ix.

2. Camille Renshaw, "Arcade, or How to Write a Novel," *Boston Review*, 1 June 1999, web.

3. Patrick Meanor, "LISH, Gordon," *The Continuum Encyclopedia of American Literature,* ed. Steven R. Serafin (New York: Continuum, 2003), 672–3 (p. 672).

4. DeLillo's remark first appeared on the jacket of Lish's novel *Zimzum* (New York: Pantheon, 1993).

5. Rust Hills, "*Esquire*'s Guide to the Literary Universe," *Esquire*, August 1987, pp. 51–62.

6. McGurl, pp. 221–222.

7. See "Lish Ash-Canned, with Perfect Civility," *New York Magazine*, 12 December 1994, p. 14.

8. Alexander Nazaryan, "An Angry Flash of Gordon," *Newsweek*, 6 September 2014, www.europe.newsweek.com/angry-flash-gordon-255491.

9. The correct quotation is "What is laid upon us is to accomplish the negative; the positive is already given." Lish almost certainly encountered it not in Kafka, but in Bloom's *Ruin the Sacred Truths* (1987), which he frequently recommended to students.

10. See John Aldridge, *Talents and Technicians: Literary Chic and the New Assembly-Line Fiction* (New York: Scribner's, 1992).

11. Gordon Lish, letter to Don DeLillo, 17 February 1987, folder 98.3, Don DeLillo MSS, the University of Texas at Austin, Harry Ransom Center.

12. George Carver, "Lish, Gordon: Notes and Reflections of a Former Student," *Pif Magazine*, 1 September 2000, www.pifmagazine.com/2000/11/lish-gordonnotes-and-reflections-of-a-former-student.

13. Gordon Lish, letter to Tom Wolfe, 13 December 1979, folder 15.2, Tom Wolfe papers, Manuscripts and Archives Division, The New York Public Library; italics in original.

14. Robert Faggen, "The Art of Fiction No. 136: Ken Kesey," *The Paris Review*, 130, Spring 1994, www.theparisreview.org/interviews/1830/ken-kesey-the-art-of-fiction-no-136-ken-kesey.

Chronology

1934　　Born February 11, in Hewlett, New York, to Philip and Regina Lish. Attends school in Lawrence, New York.

1949　　Enrolls at Philips Academy Andover, but is later expelled after an altercation with an anti-Semitic classmate. Lish's expulsion sets the pattern for his later career; as he acknowledges in this volume, "I've been fired from every job I've ever had."

1953　　Following experimental steroid treatment for psoriasis, Lish suffers a hypomanic episode, and is admitted to Bloomingdale Hospital, White Plains. Here he meets the poet Hayden Carruth, a formative influence with whom he maintains a close friendship until Carruth's death in 2008.

1954　　Embarks on a brief career as a radio personality, producing and performing on "The Gordo Lochwood Show."

1956　　Marries first wife, Loretta Frances Fokes, mother of Jennifer, Rebecca, and Ethan Lish. The two divorce in 1967.

1957　　Enrolls at the University of Arizona, majoring in English and German. Encounters the creative writing instructor Edward Loomis, initially an antagonist, but later a friend. Lish soon puts his German skills to use, penning translations of Gottfried Benn.

1959　　Moves to San Francisco, and forges important friendships with Neal Cassady, Ken Kesey, Jack Gilbert, and others.

1962　　Edits the little magazine *Genesis West* (previously *Chrysalis West*) publishing writers including Cassady, Gilbert, Kesey, Herbert Gold, Donald Barthelme, Denise Levertov, LeRoi Jones and Leonard Gardner. The magazine's eight-issue run ends in 1965.

1963　　Is fired from his first teaching post, at Mills High School, Millbrae. The incident is the subject of a front-page article in *The Nation*, "The Man Who Taught Too Well." Students include future geneticist J. Craig Venter.

1963	Is hired as Director of Linguistic Studies at Behavioral Research Laboratories, Palo Alto. Here Lish writes and edits textbooks including the two-volume *English Grammar* (1964), *Why Work* (1966) and *A Man's Work* (1967).
1969	Marries second wife, Barbara Works, mother of Atticus Lish.
1969	Becomes fiction editor at *Esquire*, adopting the soubriquet "Captain Fiction." Publishes Raymond Carver, Richard Ford, Don DeLillo, Grace Paley, Barry Hannah, James Purdy, Cynthia Ozick, Vladimir Nabokov, Norman Mailer, Saul Bellow, T. C. Boyle, Joyce Carol Oates, John Cheever, John Gardner, and many others. Lish is fired in 1976, following a conflict with *Esquire*'s new management over Ozick's story "Levitation."
1972	Begins an influential career as a creative writing instructor, initially at Yale University, and later at New York University and Columbia University. Over the decades, Lish's activities as a teacher take him to Chicago, Indiana, San Francisco, and elsewhere. His "Tactics of Fiction" class at Columbia inspires Amy Hempel's *Vanity Fair* essay, "Captain Fiction" (1984), the first of numerous magazine articles on his teaching.
1975	Begins correspondence with both his *Esquire* author Don DeLillo, and his Yale colleague Harold Bloom. Lish and DeLillo become lasting friends, reading and discussing each others' manuscripts. DeLillo's *Mao II* (1991) is dedicated to Lish. Bloom's literary theory directly informs Lish's teaching, and Lish introduces Bloom to the work of Cormac McCarthy. The two fall out over Bloom's *The Western Canon* (1994).
1977	Publishes "For Rupert—with no Promises" in *Esquire*. A parodic homage to J. D. Salinger, "For Rupert" is the first unsigned story in *Esquire*'s forty-four-year history. The national press are briefly convinced that Salinger is the author of the story.
1977	Becomes senior editor at Alfred A. Knopf. Publishes novels, short story collections, and poetry by Raymond Carver, Barry Hannah, Jack Gilbert, Mary Robison, Amy Hempel, Harold Brodkey, Anne Carson, Joy Williams, Walter Kirn, Brian Evenson, Ben Marcus, Sheila Kohler, Nancy Kaufmann, Rudy Wilson, and many others.
1983	Publishes *Dear Mr. Capote*, his first novel as "Gordon Lish" (by now, Lish is already a prolific author of ghost-written and pseudonymous novels). *Capote* is swiftly followed by

	his early masterpiece, *Peru* (1986), and over a dozen other novels and story collections.
1986	Teaches the final session of "Tactics of Fiction" at Columbia. From now on, Lish devotes himself to private instruction. Often held in students' apartments, Lish's private classes last at least six hours each, and differ sharply from the conventional "workshop" format.
1987	Founds literary magazine *The Quarterly*, publishing Jason Schwartz, Mark Richard, Sam Michel, Noy Holland, Gary Lutz, Diane Williams, Christine Schutt, Lily Tuck, Dawn Raffel, and others. Many, but not all, of *The Quarterly*'s authors are also Lish's students.
1992	Successfully sues *Harper's* for reproducing a private letter to his students.
1994	Death of Barbara Lish from Lou Gehrig's Disease. Barbara's illness and death form the subject of Lish's novel *Epigraph* (1996).
1994	Is dismissed from Knopf, during a round of staff reductions across the Random House Group. *The Quarterly* ceases publication the following year.
1995	Carol Polsgrove publishes evidence of Lish's extensive editing of Raymond Carver. Three years later, journalist D.T. Max popularizes Polsgrove's discovery in an article for the *New York Times*.
1998	Teaches the last of his private writing classes. Lish briefly re-emerges to teach at the Center for Fiction in New York City from 2009 to 2012, where he mentors a new generation of writers, including Mitchell Jackson, May-Lan Tan, Robb Todd, Kimberly King Parsons, and Matt Bell.
2010–2017	Publishes *Collected Fictions*, his first book since *Krupp's Lulu* (2000). The collection is followed by the late works *Goings* (2014), *Cess* (2015), and *White Plains* (2017).

Conversations with Gordon Lish

Gordon Lish Interviews Gordon Lish

Gordon Lish / 1965

From *Genesis West*, Winter 1965, pp. 3–10. © 1965 Gordon Lish. Reprinted by permission.

Q: Why are you consenting to this interview?
A: I have a true thing to say.

Q: You could write an essay.
A: Too fussy, too formal, too effortful. Besides which, I'm a dynamic conversationalist.

Q: You prefer this farce to an essay?
A: I have a true thing to say.

Q: Okay. What qualifies you to edit *Genesis West?*
A: If I may speak dynamically, the answer is money. I had the money to print the first issue, so I appointed myself editor-in-chief.

Q: Is the magazine still operated on your funds?
A: Listen, I never had any funds. What I had was money, enough for one issue. After that, a corporation was formed, a non-profit corporation. It's a thing literary magazines devise in order to receive funds.

Q: Is there nothing else that qualifies you to edit such a magazine?
A: Well, I've always liked to read. So long as there's a box of Uneeda Biscuits handy, I could read for hours.

Q: You figure that's enough?
A: One box? Sure, it gets me started.

Q: I mean qualification.
A: I don't know. I suppose so. I did teach fiction writing for a time, but the college fired me.

Q: They fired you?
A: I think it was because my class enrollment grew from twelve to seventy-three. It was an unhealthy environment for the students—legal occupancy, fire regulations, and so on.

Q: You were such a compelling instructor?
A: No, I *cried* easily. I would get so worked up over something I was reading as a model of good prose that I'd have to turn to the blackboard. But they could tell, anyway. I think a lot of those people came to watch me weep. Most of them were older women, you see. The ventilation in there was pretty risky for them.

Q: I take it you're quickly moved to passion.
A: That's right. I am.

Q: You are not guarded in your public statements, then?
A: No, I am not, therefore, guarded in my public statements.

Q: Suppose we test your candor.
A: I am prepared to have my candor tested.

Q: Why did you start *Genesis West*?
A: Well, I had to start something, you see. My friends were generally undistinguished. It seemed to Franny and me that if I were editing a little magazine we would meet all sorts of celebrated people.

Q: And did you?
A: Oh, yes. We met a great number of them.

Q: And was the experience satisfying?
A: Well, not exactly. Mostly, I think it depressed me.

Q: Why so?
A: I found out, you see, that the people I was meeting were also interested in making more distinguished friendships. Some of them even asked me if

I were distinguished. They'd pull that on the telephone or in a letter—never to your face.

Q: You were disenchanted?
A: Profoundly. With poets particularly.

Q: Why poets?
A: They are forever on the make, intensely so. And they can be very nasty people when you don't cooperate.

Q: In what way must you cooperate?
A: First, you must publish their poems and then you must introduce them to distinguished people. Apparently poets thrive on distinguished relationships. I think it has something to do with acquiring funds or medals. It's all very complex, really.

Q: I take it you have had some personal head-knocking with a poet.
A: Yes, I have had some personal head-knocking with a poet. If I may speak dynamically, I knocked heads with a little lady poet in New York.

Q: She was nasty?
A: Unspeakably. I failed to cooperate and she became unspeakably nasty. This little lady will threaten to ruin your sales in the East. She will call you a fascist. She will write you letters, send you telegrams, poison your water supply.

Q: Her name, the name of this poet?
A: I never knew her real name. She worked an alias. New York editors tell me she's the war counselor for a bopping gang on 7th Avenue. I have saved all her letters. They are miracles of abbreviated lower case and not infrequently contain the word "zonk."

Q: Did you print her poems?
A: Of course. She's a good poet. After a while you get used to all the other crap.

Q: There were many such people?
A: Poets like that? Dynamically-speaking, yes. There's two guys who ship you fifty poems at a crack, each of them labeled with a long numeral. I think it's some kind of code.

Q: I gather your encounters with poets have not been altogether inspiring.
A: That's right. My encounters with poets have not been altogether inspiring. I am, in fact, learning to hate poets as a group.

Q: You are, perhaps, beginning to speak a shade too dynamically?
A: Look, let me tell you about poets who teach. They submit their stuff with a list attached showing all their publishing credits. Magazines like *Armpit 5* and *The Burning Crotch*. You *know* they teach because they always include this little note on university stationery. You don't dare reject them.

Q: But poets are simply people—subjects to the same human failings that diminish us all.
A: You'll never get them to agree to it.

Q: Such a harsh judgement from such a young man!
A: Well, I told you I speak dynamically. Besides, I suffer from psoriasis and am consequently prone to irritability during the winter months. No more poets, not in *Genesis West*. Besides, there are thousands of places for poets to get their stuff in print, and damn few for prose writers.

Q: Did you say no more poets in *Genesis West*?
A: Yes, I did say no more poets in *Genesis West*. With the exception of Jack Gilbert.

Q: Is he not arrogant, too?
A: Jack? Jack is the most arrogant son-of-a-bitch who ever hoisted a pencil, but in his case the arrogance is earned. So far as I'm concerned, anyway.

Q: But you hassled with Jack Gilbert—publicly.
A: Well, you figured me for passionate and I already told you that I'm dynamic.

Q: I remember your complaining about Gilbert's arrogance when he attempted to edit poetry for *Genesis West*. You suggested he was cruel in his wholesale rejections.
A: That's right. Jack did reject them wholesale, and I did complain to him because the poets started complaining to me. I called Jack gratuitously cruel when he was simply being honest. You know what it is to deal with a man

whose standards are impeccably high? Not easy, let me tell you. Very tricky stuff. I know. When I was teaching school, I made plenty of people miserable with my impeccably high standards. I was right, unimpeachably right, but they finally had to put me out on the street. That's what I did to Jack. Bounced him out of editing our poetry because he wanted to run blank pages where mediocre poems might have occupied space. Listen, I could turn toward a blackboard when I talk about this. The man's poems are the only ones that have altered my opinion of myself. That must count for something. That must mean he's a great poet. But the man is very demanding. Like his poetry, a heavy demand, a thunderous burden. To swing with it, you must match it with your own energy, an equally heroic courage. So there's Gilbert peppering the mails with his thoughtful, painful honesty on behalf of *Genesis West* and all I wanted to accomplish were a few distinguished friendships. Too risky. We were destined to clash.

Q: And now? All is forgotten?
A: Nothing is ever forgotten, I failed him badly. We forgive but we don't forget, and the thing is irremediably changed. The best that could come of *Genesis West* would be for Gilbert to take it over, make it strictly a vehicle for poetry, and edit the hell out of it. Nothing but blank pages! Such excellence the mind could not contain it! Listen, find me somebody with money enough—funds enough—and I swear to you I'll persuade Jack to do it.

Q: A moment ago you said that there were too many showcases for poetry and not enough for prose.
A: So? I contradict myself? In addition to speaking dynamically, I also contradict. It's a matter of editorial policy with me. You want contradictions? I'll give you contradictions. Be a thorough friend to Jack Gilbert and Ken Kesey in the same life! Try loving them both! For one night listen to them both talk and agree, agree! Three weeks ago my living room was the scene of a massive contradiction! Gilbert squatting here, Kesey squatting there, me in the middle—a regular nodding machine. Jack summons up pinnacles, I stand on them! Ken shapes a wilderness, let me be the first to grab a knapsack! Gilbert calls on restraint, I grin wildly and wink my eye! Kesey apostrophizes freedom, I chortle frantically and punch his arm! Both men are geniuses. Should I deny myself the rare company of a genius? I know so many I could afford to be spendthrift? Listen, what's an editor if he can't cough up a little contradiction for friends. For genius I'd lie myself straight to the grave!

Q: But I see where this issue presents work by another poet, James Spencer. James Spencer is not, I take it, Jack Gilbert.
A: No. James Spencer is not Jack Gilbert. I won't hesitate to concur with you on that.

Q: Why are you printing his poem, then?
A: Well, James Spencer started out being a distinguished friendship. It later turned out that he wasn't exactly distinguished, but he remained a friend. A fellow can do worse than a favor for a friend now and then. Excuse me, but what else is a literary magazine for?

Q: You can say that after praising Jack Gilbert's point of view?
A: I can say anything. It's my gift. As an editor, I'm entitled.

Q: You regard yourself with some importance?
A: I am all the time trying, yes. I also encourage my wife to make the same effort.

Q: Your wife has been a help to you with the magazine?
A: Actually, she has. She taught me to speak dynamically. Franny also packed me a nice lunch when I drove to New York for the ALMA meeting last year.

Q: That's the Association of Literary Magazines of America?
A: ALMA, that's right. A phenomenon called collapse; that's how you get the word, by collapsing down to the initial letters.

Q: What ever happened to ALMA?
A: I don't know. I tried to find out, but nobody was home. My guess is the thing flopped—collapsed, if I may express myself more dynamically—and nobody wants the responsibility of saying so.

Q: You did attend one of their meetings, then?
A: Yes, I did, in fact, attend one of their meetings. I was telling you about this nice lunch Franny made up and driving . . .

Q: What was it like?
A: The bread was kind of dry, but when you've been out on that road for a couple of days . . .

Q: What was the ALMA meeting like?
A: A polite street fight. Aside from Reed Whittemore, every editor there seemed delighted with the opportunity to take a public shit on the editor he despised most. Editors, I have discovered, are even nastier than poets.

Q: Whittemore edits *The Carleton Miscellany*?
A: Correct. The only litmag I read from cover to cover.

Q: You like others, though?
A: Not so much that I would miss them, no. But I do like *Hudson,* their fiction, mostly out of loyalty for their having printed so much Ben Maddow.

Q: You have favorite writers?
A: I have favorite everything.

Q: Name some favorite writers.
A: I'll name one because it can do me some good.

Q: Go ahead.
A: Anatole Broyard!

Q: There's no one by that name.
A: I suppose not. I've got this embarrassing imagination, you know what I mean?

Q: Then I suppose you write.
A: I quit.

Q: Why so?
A: *Partisan Review* never answered my letters.

Q: I don't understand.
A: Neither did I. I had sent them this story, you see? My *best* story. So, I naturally tore up all the others because they weren't as good as my best. You want to hear a title? "Gasserpod, Gasserpod!" I confess to regarding that repetition as very dynamic, title-wise. Well, after six months I wrote those people and asked them where my story was. Every six months thereafter, I'd write another letter—a degree stronger, nastier, more ominous. I hinted at lawyers, great wealth, a litigious personality. Finally, I threatened

to ruin their sales in the West, called them fascists, plotted their water supply. Three years later now and still no answer. So I quit writing.

Q: Letters or stories?
A: Both. Now I write textbooks.

Q: I gather you are content in doing this?
A: You are right to gather that I am content in doing this.

Q: Have you already published such a book?
A: Yes, my first is called *English Grammar.*

Q: The book is selling well?
A: Precisely, but that is not the best of it.

Q: What is, as you say, the best of it?
A: I am being sought out by people eager for a distinguished friendship.

Q: Will you disappoint them?
A: They aren't entitled?

Burlingame, California

Gordon Lish

Amy Penn / 1988

Originally published in *Interview* magazine, January 1988. Courtesy BMP Media Holdings, LLC. Reprinted by permission.

Amy Penn: Where have you taught writing?
Gordon Lish: I've taught at Yale, Columbia, and NYU. Now I only teach privately. I run workshops in the spring and fall, two at a time—one meets on Tuesday nights, the other on Thursday nights—from six to twelve o'clock.

Q: Who are some of the writers who have studied with you?
A: Amy Hempel and Anderson Ferrell are two who are well known. I can tell you two names you will certainly know as the years wear on: Mark Richard and Yannick Murphy. I predict the highest returns for two others: Jennifer Allen and Ted Pejovich. While making predictions, I'll say that William Tester will be knocking you flat presently. One of my former students is Christopher Coe, and he has published his first book, a splendid novella called *I Look Divine*.

Q: Do you consider yourself first and foremost a writer or a teacher?
A: I feel most centered in myself and most useful to the world as a teacher. I feel most possessed of a kind of unpredictable exuberance when I am teaching, so that surely, to offer a quick judgment, I'd want to claim that my personality is actually that of a teacher. Writing does not leave me with the kind of enduring satisfaction that teaching does. When I am obliged to review sentences that I have put into the world, I find it difficult to continue having an affection for them. Not so for what I produce as a teacher. As a writer, the best I've done strikes me as not nearly good enough.

Q: Are there certain qualities you have found to be consistent in the writers you have taught?
A: Yes. I believe that each of these writers has widened my own purchase on the world, on my heart, on my own perception of myself moving through the world. I can't imagine my taking on a writer who in some way did not engage a visceral response matched by an intellectual response. I have to feel myself overwhelmed and opened up to visions that would not have already occurred to me. I don't look to these prospects to confirm what I already know, but rather to surprise, to unsettle, to refresh, to jog me to the side a goodish distance. So that when there comes a writer like Yannick Murphy or Mark Richard, two persons whose work could not be more unlike the kind of work I myself would produce, I'm stunned and loudly exhilarated by the prospect for extension of what I know and feel. These writers are not continuous with what my own impulses are. They occur to me as prophets to my being in the world. They enlarge my own experience rather than confirm my own experience, by persuading me that these things are in the world. These things are in the world somewhere, and I, without their guidance, would not have seen these things.

Q: Let's discuss Lish's Laws.
A: Lish's Laws seem to me almost obnoxious now, but I know I've stated them. They're evolving with the time. To be a writer, to be a teacher, one has to maintain a certain rate of growth. If not, you're not doing your work anymore. I would now revise the term laws to read something like principles, claims, or adulations.

To be a writer, one has to tell the truth, and one has to tell the hardest truth that is available in one. One has to tell one's own truth. One has to risk everything to capture that truth; one has to reach down inside of oneself to the zone of most crucial danger, to the zone where, in fact, one may even be unsettling one's notion of oneself and therefore destabilizing one's personality. Through means of acoustical pressure, through means of thematic pressure, one must extrude that acuity and get it onto the page so that it can be seen. I think that this task is accomplished chiefly as a function of courage, of the will, and then of an absolutely unrelenting industry.

If we are bent on rendering our acuity precisely as we understand it to be in our deepest, deepest selves, then I think, all things being equal, we have a very rich prospect of making an important noise in national literature. I'm only talking about the procedure—how one begins to elucidate a story, to find a story in oneself, a story of such rank as to merit the attention of persons who are all day long confronted with the shrieks of humanity. As we come to the end of the century, how does one properly engage intelligent attention in a world that is screaming for excellent reason into the ears of everyone out there all day long? How does one make, within that frame, a noise of the kind that warrants the attention of one's proper audience? One has to find in oneself the place of greatest jeopardy, and then with a kind of surfeit of recklessness and courage, go beyond even that to uncover yet another kind of disqualifying and contradicting truth. The writer must each time redouble his efforts to probe more deeply, and more deeply and more deeply, knowing that as he does so he gains the fuel, the energy for an important fictional discourse. It is the only way for a writer to confront the horrific discouragement of being in a world with people who are smarter than he is, who know more, who feel more, who have more, who have had more experience and who will again and again surpass him in capturing attention. It seems to me that one must come to terms with the interior object and find one's stories within it.

Q: Let's touch on the method to your madness. You'll throw anything from a student's divorce to his bank account in his face. Do you have any idea of how some of your students leave your classroom and what you may have evoked in them?

A: Yes. I don't think anyone leaves untouched or unaffected. I think some go away ultimately disapproving, ultimately undone; many go away with at least a way of thinking about writing, an attitude toward being an artist. I think that an increasingly remarkable share of these students are able to go away with a strong sense of what is requisite for the page. People have transformed themselves within a matter of two or three meetings. At the same time, I've observed persons who have been with me for four, five, six workshops—that is to say many, many hours of the most vehement instruction—who are probably worse off than when they came to me, because what they had, what they believed in, has been taken from them, and nothing has been put in its place. Which is not to say that I have not put anything in its place, but rather I claim that such persons have been unable to install anything in its place. I think that inability is frequently a function of age. The older we get, the more difficult it is to take on new ways of behaving, and that's largely what my kind of teaching is about. It's about another way to behave. If by a certain age you've gotten through life managing your environment with a certain relation to language, it is extraordinarily difficult to set that aside, and that's really what's required. So sometimes it seems to me the younger candidates make the better students.

Q: You've said that if you're going to write, you're going to write. You're going to write at three in the morning, you're going to write if you're half asleep . . .

A: Absolutely. Even without the search for an alibi for failing to write—funeral services for a family member, illness—the body, your own body, wants you to fail, and it will always offer up alibis for you to fail. I think one makes this a daily oblation; it's an undertaking that must be habitual in the face of every kind of worldly interference from spouses or children or colleagues. None of us lives in the world alone. So in order to establish the kind of discipline that is requisite to doing important writing, one has to be prepared to anger a lot of people a lot of the time, because one is obliged again and again to say, "No, I must be in my space now and do what I do in that space."

I cannot believe that anything important is earned without not only great strife for oneself, but also great rupture around one. It's a question of making these choices. What are you willing to pay? I believe you've got to pay through the nose in order to achieve the kind of speech that will matter in history. Because the faculty for writing is like a muscle; if it is not exercised regularly and to its stress point, it will never be a healthy muscle. You have to do this kind of thing without cease, whatever the claims on your attentions. You have to exploit yourself as insistently and as dangerously as you can, and you have to be comparably prepared to exploit everything around you. No one is claiming that the modality of the artistic life is an admirable one or even one which is suffused with civic goodness. On the contrary, it may be that the process of creating art of a kind that will have a life in history will necessarily interfere very astringently with the processes of living life. I think that's a rather fair exchange, not an unholy one at all. It is a liaison that establishes a sort of demon in the self. One has to want this greatly.

I believe that we all want to stick out in the world, that the least of us has a profound impulse to distinguish himself from everyone else on earth, and I believe the doing of art—creativity—is the way we chiefly go about this kind of thing. The bulk of us are deprived of such opportunities. If we are determined to stick out to such extremes as to be given account of in history, then the price for doing so is going to be exorbitant.

Q: What are your expectations for yourself as a writer?

A: I have a collection of short stories called *Mourner at the Door* coming out in March. But what I want to write is *Extravaganza,* a novel I've been working on for six years. I want it to be a novel that brings to the page the configuration of the most secret pressure in me. In the last twelve versions that I've written of this book, I've discovered that I have yet to uncover that pressure. I'm well aware of what it is, but I'm yet to have the grip on it to be able to put it down. I keep teasing around the edges of it, then tart it up to make it handsomer, more genial, more congenial. In the version I'm beginning now, the only real challenge is to be the equal to what I know the task must be. It is not really a challenge that is literary, because I have the means to do the work. I know how to make the sentences. I have to find the courage to utter those sentences. As of a week or so ago, I did not have the courage, but this morning I believe I do.

Q: Where does that courage come from?
A: It comes in part from recklessness, part from fearlessness, part from desire and part, I think, from the will to dissolve the self. If you want badly enough what all of us want—to dissolve oneself, to fall out of time, to fall out of history, to swoon—then you may be willing to let go of ego just long enough to have something which appears to be courage. I think that if you are enough overcome by that feeling, you may, for a bit of time, be willing to let go of your vanity, your shame, your ego, so that you can dissolve with an audience watching. That's what I want.

Q: Let's talk about the new magazine that you're editing.
A: I have persuaded the key officers at Random House to back me in a literary magazine, an adventure that is called *The Quarterly*. As an activity, it brings to a kind of closure a tremendous impulse in me, which is to find ways to shout about that for which I have great affection. The magazine represents an extraordinarily open forum for the unsigned and undiscovered who are writing in English. I hope to claim that I've been discovering a great, great number of them each time we come out. What I'm doing is singing as loud as I can my praises for them. I can't begin to tell you how greatly I am restored by this activity.

Q: Do you think that anything exists for writers in New York that is "homey"?
A: That is homey in the sense of community? I'm not really able to answer this question with accuracy because of my age. I can think of a number of networks where young writers come together, sometimes socially, sometimes professionally, that must give them some sense of being in communion with one another. Given my age and my isolation, I have such a feeling

of fellowship with a group of writers, and we often are in touch with each other. These would be Don DeLillo, Cynthia Ozick, Harold Brodkey chiefly. It would be extended to Harold Bloom and Denis Donoghue. These are people with whom I'll have some regular intercourse—by telephone, over lunch—but nothing that would constitute the regular contact that I think younger artists do have and do require and should profit from. I'm not willing to believe that writers of my age are necessarily improved by such contact on an intense basis. My hunch is that it is a diversion from activities they should most probably be at. One must rid oneself of alibis if one wants to do this kind of work. I don't know if I can talk to someone coherently in the course of writing a novel, and I find myself distracted all the time. A novel might take a year or take me eight months or something of that sort. I'm incessantly distracted. The only time I find myself really focused in contradistinction of that distraction is when I'm teaching. It's very difficult for me to draw myself from it otherwise, so that my spouse and my children, I'm sure, pay a certain price. My friends definitely do, because I'm not in touch and not available for friendship in the way that one would like to be. If I think about the writers I admire most, they tend to be isolated. They tend not to need or wish for the company of others very much. One's family seems to be about the size of it.

Q: Is writing lonely?
A: Writing isn't lonely in the most important sense, because when you do it, you are in touch with your best friend, so the loneliness can be abridged in those terms. Also, a writer can suppose to himself that by doing his work, he is fashioning a bridge to other lone souls in space and in time—that he is in conversation with the most secret place in himself and others. I am most willing to sense a kind of consort when I am truly engaged in a conversation with my deepest self. I then feel as if I'm Gordon Lish. Gordon and not even Lish. As if I'm Gordy. As if I'm suddenly emptied of all the impediments that interfered with my having access to Gordy: my age, the world I live in, the lies I tell all day long, all the fraudulences in the world that make life doable, of which we all are immeasurably guilty. I'm not entirely convinced that the routine complaint of loneliness really suffices to answer the entire question. Of course, you do it by yourself. You can't even count on anyone else in your immediate camp to put up with the sort of behavior you create around you when you are doing this sort of thing. You really ought not to ask anyone into it; you oughtn't to read to your spouse or your children or your parents and so on. I think that you go into the bathroom and you do your business.

Captain Fiction:
Super-Teacher Gordon Lish

Gail Caldwell / 1988

From *The Boston Globe*, 7 March 1988, p.17. © 1989. Boston Globe Media Partners. All rights reserved. Used by permission and protected by the Copyright Laws of the United States. The printing, copying, redistribution, or retransmission of this Content without express written permission is prohibited.

NEW YORK—Gordon Lish—writer, teacher, editor—is giving a reading as part of a cultural series at noon to a Wall Street crowd, which couldn't seem more incongruous: If the man believes his own colleagues find him "too much," what's the three-piece-suit set going to think? But Lish is a man of chameleonic charm, and he shows up early wearing a dramatic leather duster and full-slouch, wide-brim hat. Underneath, for the podium, is a tweed suit and polka-dot bow tie. Today, Lish looks more like an Oxford don than an author of scatological prose.

And he is both endearing and stately as he addresses this small audience. Listening to Lish woo the bankers and bond salesmen who've wandered into Chase Manhattan Plaza, it's easy to imagine him in the diverse roles he's held in the past four decades: radio announcer (in Pampa, Texas, in the '50s), "Jewish cowboy" (on an Arizona dude ranch, where he went for his health), literary gadfly on the West Coast (during San Francisco's early boho days). Born in New York in 1934, he was a high school dropout who later finished college in two years. He has suffered from psoriasis all his life and was hospitalized for the condition only two months ago. He says he had a daily habit of three packs of cigarettes and a bottle of booze for most of his adult life, until he gave up both five years ago, "when I had a scare." This is not a man who has led an uneventful life, or a pastoral one.

Lish is reading from his new collection, *Mourner at the Door*, and he begins by quoting the advance reviews from *Publishers Weekly* and *Kirkus*, both negative in the extreme. This has the ironic but intended effect of softening his audience, and he goes on to three of the strongest (and least offensive) stories, all first-person: a boy winning the sports events at summer camp, a man's bleak memories of his father's recent funeral, a "cold-sober" testimony of a social evening gone darkly awry. There is polite, if restrained, applause, even a little laughter; only one person has walked out in medias res. But a young woman in the back seems dismayed and raises her hand: "Where does this attitude come from? You're reducing life to its barest, ugliest minimum."

"What did you find ugly?" Lish shoots back. "You mean 'ugly,' in the sense that all of the people in this room are not going to die?"

It's pure Lish: mildly adversarial, quick on his feet, partial to theatrical observations about the human condition. He tells the woman his hope is "to be a recording angel," and he looks the part—tweedy suit, horn-rims—while last night he was all bluff and palaver, the hip patriarch of letters. But how can you not trust a guy who reads his worst possible press to a room full of pin-striped strangers?

Squeezed into a crowded car on the IRT back to midtown, Lish is holding forth on the past forty years—his first wife, his psoriasis, that radio job in Pampa. But he's also surveying the other passengers as he talks, and one can't help thinking about "The Traitor"—his unsettling story about a man on the Lexington line, and his fantasy of a machine-gun-toting assassin who gets off at 33rd. We bail out at 50th, around the corner from his office at Knopf.

This is probably what Lish's fiction does best: jab you in the rib cage during the most average of moments, illuminate the darker corners where repressed fantasy meets banal desire. It is an authorial voice few people can love, whether the serial-murderer narrator of *Dear Mr. Capote*—police called Lish after the book was published, seeking advice—or the protagonist named Gordon in *Peru*, who confesses in a long, neurosis-laden soliloquy to having killed a playmate at the age of six. In *Mourner at the Door*, the narrator vacillates between repetitive cliché and linguistic calisthenics, often burying his version of the truth amid the sordidness of life.

Lish's office, on the 21st floor, holds a small desk covered with mail, and shelves of his authors' books; there's a chess set in the window overlooking Manhattan, and photographs of the writers he reveres. After using his voice for six hours teaching the night before—he says he always talks the entire session of the first class—and reading today for almost two, the man known as Captain Fiction seems indefatigable; indeed, it's difficult to derail him even for a moment. Lish roams easily among the subjects that intrigue him, from junk language and the homogenized modern world to the failings of American fiction ("If Borges were American, we'd probably dismiss him"). Again and again he returns to the three writers he holds most dear, to whom *Mourner at the Door* is dedicated: Harold Brodkey, Cynthia Ozick, and Don DeLillo. But he is unstoppable on the subject of teaching, and he speaks of his students as though "A Clean, Well-Lighted Place" or "The Dead" were only a synapse or two away.

"I despise the elitism that surrounds the notion of the literary figure," says Lish. "What I try to produce in my students is the conviction that they are entitled—that they can seize the page with as much force and majesty and beauty as anyone else speaking. I, on the one hand, am prepared to say to people, 'Yes, I guarantee it's in you.' But I can tell you that the leap from conviction to putting yourself in an intimate relation with yourself—and with the language—is a long, long leap. It requires remarkable endurance, astounding stamina.

"I try to say to them, 'Let me see if together we can recover the voice that was in you when you didn't know how, so ably, to put words together—when you weren't so adroit, so adept, so glib.' Most persons don't want to make that leap with you. They will tell you that they do. But once they see what's involved, they'll not be able to."

Lish says he takes teaching far more seriously than any other aspect of his work. "When I teach, I'm tampering with their lives. And I'm somebody who, given my experience in this world, has a general contempt for psychiatrists, or people who take other people's lives and finger them in ways that could be disastrous. So I bank on my instinct to be responsive to what is put before me in a way that is just and inspired—a way that is on the money every time.

"It's an awful gamble. I think I'm very gifted at it. If I've not been, if I've made mistakes, then they are truly sins of mine. I would like to feel I haven't made mistakes, at least of a great magnitude. I can tell you that everything depends on my not making those mistakes.

"I try to admit my frailties, but I also think I have a kind of genius for seeing into certain texts. They tend to count on my being reliable. If I'm in any way off the mark, it's a disaster for us all. A terrible disaster."

I ask Lish about the criticism that there's a certain Lish affect or aesthetic, one that might discourage a young Faulkner or Melville—someone who writes full-throttle, old-fashionedly ornate sentences instead of the "byte-sized perceptions" of which the Lish school has been accused. He is adamant on this subject and speaks with the same conviction evident in his classes.

"I tell you this," says Lish. "This is an awful thing to say in any kind of public setting, but I honestly believe that there is an energy in me, a kind of center, which is uncanny in this regard. I wish I had it working more for me as a writer. I do feel that I wouldn't make that mistake. But if I did, I would be the worst shit in the world—because I'm so emphatic in my opinion.

"But no one is infallible. Clearly I have or will have or am already doing awful, awful things. I pray God I'm not. I pray God I somewhat am apart from all that, and am infallible, knowing all the time that I couldn't conceivably be. But I'm always prepared to be proved wrong. The awful thing about the subject we're discussing is that there is no proof. You can damage somebody and that person can close up and go away and never effloresce in the fashion one might have.

"It's a pressure cooker. It's very tough for it to be otherwise. Some people profit from that; others are destroyed by it. It's tough on me. I'm as available to measure as anybody in the room. I'm also a writer, and there are persons in those rooms who can write rings around me. They're twenty or thirty years my junior, and they can take sentences and do more with them than I ever dreamed of."

With his published writers often turning out bare-cupboard prose marked by a fragmentary vision, Lish is often credited with (or blamed for) the minimalist rage in contemporary fiction. It's a responsibility he wholeheartedly rejects.

"I'm blamed for everybody who writes short sentences," says Lish. "It is nonsense. I refuse to accept the honorific that I am in some way the dean or godfather of the contemporary short story. I published a lot of short stories at *Esquire*, when people didn't want to publish short stories. And I started publishing them here at Knopf, so in that context alone can I be seen as responsible for the renaissance, or renascence, of short stories. Indeed, a lot of them are getting published now. But I am not responsible for a certain style of writing.

"I do find it essential to hold the writers I publish to the necessity of fielding a logical discourse. Now that's not minimalism; that's something else. I really believe that when we hear the bulk of complaints about minimalism, what we're really hearing is a lot of old farts—largely writers who have been superannuated by the younger writers—who are somehow crying 'Foul! Foul!'"

Lish's guru status might not raise so many eyebrows if his own writing were more mainstream, or at least less concerned with the noisome pockets of existence. With its weird, cliché-ridden monologues, its laundry-list epiphanies and shockers (one story concerns a couple who begins each day by throwing up), *Mourner at the Door* is sure to surprise or discourage even a few Lish believers. The strongest story in the collection is a kind of anti-Christ metaphor, plagued by damaged children and bumbling, cruel adults. But Lish defends his fiction as simply recording "the drama that surrounds us," arguing that he tries to undercut the sadness of his stories with wry or ironic effect.

"I think when most people pick up a book," says Lish, "they want to take a pill and go away somewhere. And I don't want to be the one to provide the pill. I want to be the one who says: 'You can look at what is revealed here, you can live with it, it isn't so awful. Contrarily, you'll find much in it that is majestic, even transcendent, if you can live with life as it is.'

"I don't want my books to be ugly. I want in some way to celebrate diversity, the rhythm of life, with no shirking, no shying away. I don't want to make ugliness; my God, nothing could be further from my spirit. I'm evidently a man who tries to surround myself with beauty whenever I can. I see these stories as really beautiful.

"Truly, truly, if one can find four or five good readers—then I'm happy as a clam. I don't expect to be liked by a lot of people. I just don't want my neighbors to throw rocks through my windows. And they don't do that, so I feel that I'm getting away with murder!" Lish laughs. "But I never expected to go into the country club and be lifted up on the shoulders of all my golfmates, and be carried out onto the green."

That's not a scenario likely to happen soon. Lish seems to move alone through his insular literary world. A fey, engaging man, he is given to dramatic analogy—someone who, in conversation, interrupts constantly with bursts of "Yes, yes, yes, absolutely, oh right!" He is almost painfully self-aware, and seems resigned to the discomforts of this life, calling his writing "my church, my psychiatrist." And he believes unflinchingly in his gift for the writers of tomorrow. That certitude, more than any four-letter-word blows against the empire, is what makes Gordon Lish such anathema to his detractors—and what keeps writers from Tacoma to the East Village lining up for a glance at the Grail.

Captain Fiction Rides Again: The Further Adventures of Gordon Lish

Lisa Grunwald / 1989

Previously published in Esquire *magazine, March 1989. Reprinted with the permission of Lisa Grunwald.*

What he says when I walk in the door
"Here. Read this. I gotta go *pish.*"

What he has handed me
Three new books of fiction, just edited by him at Alfred A. Knopf, and a twenty-page manuscript filled with anger and one-sentence paragraphs. One-sentence paragraphs mark a lot of the fiction he edits—a stark, experimental genre that was called the New Fiction when he pioneered it here at *Esquire* back in the 1970s.

What he is, anyway
Ubiquitous. Skinny. Devoted. Fast. Brilliant. Exhausting. Nuts. Editor (at Knopf). Teacher (of two six-hour classes a week). Author (of *Peru, Dear Mr. Capote, Extravaganza,* all written with a style part Joyce, part Salinger, part Jackie Mason). For the last two years, he's also been the sole editor of a new literary magazine he founded called *The Quarterly*. His nickname is Captain Fiction. Of course, he *gave* himself the nickname. But after two decades playing jester, cajoler, guru, champion, scold, father, friend, and hypnotist to a flock of eager writers, he's definitely grown into it.

Why this article is being written in this form
Because to speak of Gordon Lish is to speak to a three-way mirror that is constantly throwing off images at all sorts of crazy slants and angles, and no straightforward narrative seems to apply to him.

What he says when he walks back in
"Okay, pal. Right. Yes. Yes. Right."

What decorates his office
Photographs of his wife and son. Framed covers of *The Quarterly*, a few cartoons, pictures of Ernest Hemingway and Truman Capote, a reading stand instead of a desk, and a backdrop of dusty, mirrored windows.

Writers he has published (a very partial list)
Don DeLillo, Milan Kundera, Gabriel García Márquez, Ken Kesey, Truman Capote, Barry Hannah, Nancy Lemann, Amy Hempel, Harold Brodkey, Raymond Carver, Denis Donoghue, Cynthia Ozick.

A fairly typical sentence
"I think no few writers who are already emerged writers have the word that they might not be received with such hospitality at *The Quarterly*, and they're not inclined to I think volunteer themselves for a no."

What it means
He'd rather publish unknowns.

Why?
"One woman in my class stopped writing at seventeen and is now thirty-five. All the plaque that plants itself in the heart and in the mouth and indeed in the hand had not presented itself in her case. She came to the page with a whole new set of suppositions that were a product of the pressure of the moment rather than a kind of learned way of being on the page."

What about the buzz that would come from publishing, say, Norman Mailer's next work?
"I don't want it, I don't want it, I don't want it, I don't want it."

Oh, come on
"I really don't think that there *is* such a buzz. Not, certainly, among the constituency that supports *The Quarterly*. I think it's probably largely a generation that would not feel Mailer's next interventions on the page would be all that thrilling to behold."

What *The Quarterly* offers instead
Thirty to forty new works (mostly fiction, with some poetry) in a shiny trade paperback that comes out with the seasons. Lish boasts that *The Quarterly* receives one-hundred-and-fifty to two hundred submissions a day and has, with a circulation of twelve thousand to fifteen thousand, already surpassed its much older competitors. He looks at every submission himself, usually within a day, pays next to nothing when he accepts a piece, and when he turns one down, sends a rejection note that is nearly as profound as some of the stories he takes.

Why it's so hard to write
"I believe that one can be in the most purged of solitudes and still be terribly, terribly alert to oneself as an actor. You know, one washes one's face and as one does so one makes a face in the mirror. One is constantly pulling faces, even for God. And I think that what we're talking about is a way to get rid of one's face."

His face
Is framed by white hair that is thinning; is centered by a birdish nose, deepened by craggy skin. But mostly his face is the shock of his lips, which never stop moving, and of his eyes, which never stop shining.

The major enemies of great fiction

> Fear: "That's why so many writers drink or take drugs. It's fear, it's fear, it's fear, it's fear, it's embarrassment, it's anxiety, it's fear, it's fear."
> Self-consciousness: "One has to find a way to uncover the heart."
> Money: "If I can't outpull everyone else as a function of my alacrity as an editor, I quit. I don't want to make this magazine the best it can be simply as a function of Knopf having very deep pockets."
> Hollywood: "But of course anybody who volunteers himself for that sort of whoredom gets exactly what he's set up for. We all open our legs for something."

Speaking of which
No, I won't ask him about all the Svengali stories.

What I will ask him
Is whether he doesn't have, as an editor, the temperament of the seducer, constantly falling in love with first work and never worrying about whether he'll see a writer through to the end.

His first response
"Guilty as charged. Guilty as charged. I do not feel any kind of fealty to the writer that extends beyond the text. The work has always had to be as robust for me the fifth time out as it was the first time. Does this mean that my perception of the degree of its robustness diminishes as 'I have my way' with it? Mayhaps."

On second thought
"I like the symmetry of the analogy, but maybe I'm not that awful. Hell, I've been sobbing with one writer now for several years to bring to the page a novella he's been working on. But am I as aroused by that as to be publishing someone who's brand-new to me? No, I'm guilty as charged."

What's the fantasy?
"Daryl Scroggins from Dallas, Texas. Never heard of this fellow. No letter. No nothing. With a name that would suggest anything but the kind of text that was on the page, which was a joy to receive. I got a letter off to him straightaway saying "Send me everything you've ever written, I simply adore you, I adore you." That's the ideal. Ideally he'll have twenty stories of that kind, and I'll publish a collection. And then what? Then, you would say, I'll wear him out, wear him out, so that Daryl Scroggins ends up being published by some other house? Is that the ideal case? Yes, maybe. But I hope not. I would clearly hope that Daryl Scroggins would reach down, pick the carpet up, put it in his pocket, and walk away with the whole thing."

Who can get the whole thing
"Writers who take the view that the world is what we make it and then are eager to make it something. Writers who believe that the statements at the opening of Genesis can be applied to themselves, and that when they come to the page, the pencil in their hands is a magic wand."

What it takes
"It's a matter of wanting. It's a matter of not only wanting but of believing."

Where does that come from, for him?
"The truth? It doesn't anymore. I feel vacant. It's easy to feel vacant when you're fifty-five. I have always had a rich family life, and I have a great partnership with my spouse, and that takes up a good deal of the slack. But undeniably my creative energies have always been at the center of me, and to feel them dissipated, to feel them exhausted is a great disappointment."

How convincing was this speech?
Very.

How moving?
Extremely.

How true?
Who knows?

What his mind is on now
The writing class that he's on his way to teach, which will start with exhortations and end at midnight.

What he puts on his head
An actual scoutmaster's hat.

How it looks
Terrific.

What he says before he rushes off into the rain
"Sorry I'm so *fartootst*. Gotta go, Tootsie. Gotta go, pal. Gotta rush."

Feeling Uniformly Jewish:
An Interview with Gordon Lish

Mario Materassi / 1990

From *Intertextual Identity: Reflections on Jewish-American Artists,* ed. by Franco La Polla and Gabriela Morisco (Bologna: Patron Editore, 1997), pp. 29–38. © 1997 Patron Editore. Reprinted by permission.

Mario Materassi: You have said that you feel first a Jew and then the man Gordon Lish. Would you care to elaborate on this?
Gordon Lish: I feel myself uniformly Jewish. I feel that whatever presence it is that animates me is more Jewish than it is informed by the name Gordon Lish or by my citizenship as an American or my status as a father or as a husband or as an editor, as well as a writer. No, I feel, for reasons that I certainly would not be competent to explain, that my sense of myself as a being is inextricably Jewish, that I only breathe because I am Jewish and that I will die because I am Jewish, that it will not require the action of Jew-haters to bring me to an end because I am Jewish, but that my insertion into existence, that my destiny in coming to the end of that existence, is not a Jewish matter but a Jewish energy. I can't really find a way to formulate the feeling that underlies the words I am now putting before you, but I can tell you that this feeling in me has never been one I have been ignorant of. It is the only reality behind all the fictions. All else in me is a fiction. So that for me to entertain the question of how I feel about myself as a Jewish writer is a kind of absurdity inasmuch as the only authenticity I feel is my Jewishness, whereas my behavior as a writer is all fraudulence, as is all my other, less necessary behavior. I'm drinking a coffee with you and I drink this coffee as a Jew, you see. Everything I do I do as a Jew. At what point in my consciousness did this sense of myself enter in? Was it the result of my having grown up during the Second World War? Was it the result of being witness to my mother and

father's difference from the persons they encountered? I can only say that as far back as I can remember, which is really a recollection of childhood games in the backyards of other children, I was keenly, I was inescapably, I was profoundly alert to a difference between certain other children and myself, and that difference somehow had to do with my Jewishness. I know that as I am alert to the sentence that I am now uttering, the unreason of the utterance is not lost on me. But I want very eagerly to respond earnestly to your question. I am making my way with—without reason.

Q: Was the difference you felt due to the way your family expressed its Jewishness vis-à-vis the others, or was it something inside you?
A: Entirely inside, entirely, I would claim, entirely proclaimed out of some interiority. My family was Jewish in their conduct but only in the most indifferent way. I was not schooled as a Jew. I did not have a religious education. I certainly did not live a life that was inflicted with Jewish symbols. I knew that I was a Jew quite without anyone having to tell me. Now that we are on the occasion of trying to find in this exchange between us some kind of plausible style of talking about this, it may be that what I am trying to say is that I always felt different, and that this "differentness" that I felt I named Jewishness. As early as I can remember, I suffered keenly the violation of my interiority, as I was obliged to confront what was exterior to me, as every child does. In my case, I assigned the word "Jew" to the gap, or to the discontinuity, between my interior and all objects exterior to myself. So that when I say to you now, at age fifty-six, that I feel myself more uniformly Jewish than I feel myself even the man Gordon Lish, I am probably saying that I feel myself the outlaw, I feel myself someone apart from others. I feel myself someone whose capacities to manage his environment, to cope with everything exterior to himself, is always a struggle, an enormous struggle, a struggle in which as my years accumulate and as my strengths diminish, both psychological and physical, I lose. So that I am increasingly alert to my difference or my apartness, and I am therefore more alert to myself as a Jew and become more and more vocal about this apartness. And I think of what I was remarking earlier, that is to say, that I do not believe that those persons who would represent themselves as central citizens in a Jewish community would regard me as Jewish, that that apartness I feel is best understood in those terms. I feel as excluded by Jews as I do by everybody else. It's not that I feel welcomed into a Jewish community by reason of my pronouncing myself Jewish or being vocal about my Jewishness. On the contrary, I do not. I can enumerate for you times when I have been programmatically,

systematically excluded from Jewish affairs by official Jews, in the very same way that I would be excluded by the official representatives of the literary community.

Q: Because you are not playing according to the rules.
A: Yes. I don't belong to Pen; I don't belong to any of the organizations—

Q: You don't go by the official symbols.
A: Absolutely not. And it's not really—I'm delighted to get this on the record with someone—it is not because I elect to play by a different set of principles. I am really incompetent to play by any others than the ones that are put before me. I wouldn't know how to do it. I wouldn't know how to join. I wouldn't know how to be a part of any kind of organization whose objectives were not my own. This would not be feasible for me as a natural enterprise. It is extraordinary to me that in the light of this dysfunction, of this disability, I should have been able to conduct a career that has been at certain points lived within this community: I work at a respectable publishing house and I've had this job for fifteen years. Prior to that time, I was an editor at a slick national magazine. It's not as if I have lived on the fringe of the world.

Yet, as would be both reported by my detractors and certainly acknowledged by me, at no point have I a history of "going along with." And my idea of myself as a Jew is concerned with that inability "to go along with." My claim is that a Jew is a dissenter. My idea of Judaism, at its most superlative formation, which is not dissonant with Harold Bloom's notions, I believe, is that it is by saying "no," it is by refusing, that I most properly acquit myself as a Jew. It is my inability or unwillingness to sanction the exteriority and its principles that, I feel, makes me very specifically a Jew. But by reason of my own definition, I certainly cannot claim to any kind of participation in a Jewish community or a Jewish religion.

When I wrote the essay that appears in *Congregation,* which is a collection of essays on the so-called Jewish Bible, my essay was an adversarial one. A young liberal rabbi asked to interview me for a radio broadcast. He was much concerned with my ideas and said that they seemed to him to be consonant with those of a heretical rabbi of the fourteenth century.

Q: Which book did you comment upon?
A: I said I would take any book that no one else wanted. I took Chronicles, and indeed after they published my essay they assigned to a rabbi the job of

indeed doing an essay on Chronicles. I, in fact, did not speak to Chronicles. But my point is that this young rabbi who was eager to discuss with me my ideas, did so, but the broadcast never aired! They did not air the broadcast! I don't know why it is that my position in these matters seems so antithetical to reason. The only official Jew that has ever discussed these matters with me is Cynthia Ozick, and she has a difficult time, I think, both acknowledging my point of view and appreciating it. She said to me at the conclusion of her reading of both those essays, the one in *Congregation* and the one in *Testimony*, "Well, I think I know what you are getting at." She certainly does not endorse my position.

If I can cite any Jew who has read these works and has offered a general agreement, it would be Harold Bloom. A writer of mine, Bette Howland, a Jewish writer who lives down in Pennsylvania, wrote me a quite lovely letter about the essay in *Testimony*, saying that she thought that it was easily the most surpassing, transcendent piece of writing she had ever read. But, I can tell you, most persons look at that essay and think it's absolute madness, and the expressions that have been used to describe it are "scatological," "obscene," "infuriating," "insulting," and so on. So that what I am getting at is that I would wish to proclaim two things: one, in respect of myself, it is the displacement between myself and what is exterior to myself that I give the name "Jew"; and then I move from that point and I take that sense of displacement, that sense of being proscribed by the normative culture, and then turn it into a philosophy, saying Judaism really ought to be, as I understand it, the conduct of an outlaw principle. That is to say, it should always say "No," it should always say "I will not consent." And I am willing to believe (I may have talked myself into this over the course of the years) that what speaks to me most deeply, in my own sense of Judaism, my Jewishness rather, is that in my interpretation of events, of objects, I come forward with a negative principle. I would cite for you the statement of Kafka which I use, as I believe, in *Extravaganza*: "the positive is already given, and it remains to us to accomplish the negative." I didn't say that latter part in *Extravaganza*, but I feel entirely that this is not just my role in life, this is my *lot* in life. I can do no other. I have four children, and I am easily prepared to cite among them those that I regard as Jewish and those that I regard as not Jewish, based entirely on my mad scheme of those who will interpret events and find that the events as delivered to our existence by reason of the exterior culture, they will interpret them as unsatisfactory, as requiring revision, as requiring reversal, as requiring overturning.

And now I hear myself playing right into the hands of John Murray Cuddihy. I don't know if you have ever read his remarkable book. He is a professor of sociology at Hunter and he has a theory that he has put forth—I don't know if he has put it forth in quite the terms that I will but it is largely encompassed in his book *The Ordeal of Civility*, in which he says that Jews, because of their having been suppressed and kept apart from the dominant culture, are animated by reason of an ambition to insert themselves into the dominant culture, and once having made at least some kind of entry therein, wish to overturn it because it has indeed proscribed them. It is not an implausible position. He then goes on to state rather persuasively how Freud, Marx, Einstein, and various other Jewish thinkers have indeed been animated by the impulse to overturn. Of course it's really the impulse of the modern, as we are fed up with the belated, the bedecked objects and we want to purge these and begin anew. In any event, I should offer the observation that Ozick, when confronted with that argument, I don't think she answers it quite successfully, but she does say, "On the contrary, it is we Jews in whom the orders of civility repose; we are the ones who invented civilization—and indeed we do not feel ourselves prevented from having the conducts, the behaviors of civility; *we* confer them on others." I think she's wrong.

Q: Maybe the two arguments can coexist because we are talking about two different levels of experience.
A: Exactly, precisely. That's certainly the case, and I may be giving unfair representation of both positions in any event. I would say, certainly about my own experience, or as I would assign Jewishness to my children, as I was saying, I feel that it is in resisting the ordinary, in resisting that which is central to the dominant position, that I define myself as a Jew. I see this in my children, and I will set them apart from one another in respect to this ... not "revolutionary," that's not exactly what it is, but a resistive personality.

Q: The capacity to dissent?
A: The capacity to dissent and to be unafraid to stand alone.

Q: Do you feel an instinctive empathy for dissenters in general, independently of your background?
A: I must say this: this is really the double bind, if you want, in which one is caught up. Neither could I join myself to the orders of dissenters, you see. And I have characteristically, over the course of my life, when been offered invitations by formal dissenters, dissented from taking up instructions, as

it were. I, perversely or divinely, am unable to do other than stand alone. I have a great feeling of concord and of fraternity with Harold Bloom, for example, on matters of a spiritual kind and matters of an intellectual kind. I have enormous respect for Denis Donoghue, who represents an entirely opposing principle from Bloom's principle. But if Bloom were to say to me, "Gordon, I have assembled a group of persons who are of like mind, we ought to meet once a week," I would find it so disabling!

Q: I would not have the time—
A: I would not have the time! Indeed, that's how I have conducted the affairs of my life. I really have the most paltry social existence. I see hardly anyone. I do not belong to any professional organizations. Increasingly I feel at a distance from my fellows. I don't regard this with contentment at all. I regard this as a most unsavory existence.

Q: My previous question was not intended to find out whether you are a card-carrying member of any dissenting organization. I was attempting to get at your sense of the relationship between being a dissenter and being a Jew. The self-portrait that you have been sketching out is mostly that of a loner, a dissenter, and not necessarily that of a Jew. Or is it? Are you saying that you are a Jew because you are a dissenter or that you are a dissenter because you are a Jew?
A: I understand. I must say, too, that some of my great American models for this kind of conduct are not Jews. Ralph Waldo Emerson would be a signal one and he, of course, is not Jewish. But I would also cite Kafka, I would cite Freud as very, very important persons from whom one takes one's instructions. But I am not a scholar in these matters and if you said to me, "Well, Gordon, your thought is preposterous. If I would put before you the details of Freud's life you would see that he was, on the contrary, scarcely an outlaw but eager, eager in every kind of way, to be just the opposite of an outlaw," I would tell you this: none of what I am saying to you issues to me as the result of any kind of ideation. I make these verbal formulations only out of trying to be an observer of what already is a fact of my life. And so when you said that what I have been doing is offering a self-portrait, you are on the mark. That's exactly it. I am simply sitting here trying to say, "Well, this is how it has worked out for me." It has always been the case, Mario, *always*, that the feelings that I have put before you as earnest ones, as authentic ones, I seem to feel that I have been aware of from the earliest times, and that the assignment that I have made to those feelings—Jewishness—also

seems to have been one that was understood by me from earliest times. And I must insist: I grew up in a very, very non-Jewish kind of way. I went to public school, where most of the students were not Jewish; I attended church to go along with one of my teachers who was fond of me and took me to church with her when I was in secondary school; I sang in the church choir; I attended church every day, which was a part of the school's procedure, but I went willingly and enjoyed all that activity. I felt myself, when I was in my mid-twenties, early thirties, on the verge of becoming a priest, an Episcopalian priest. In fact, I had been offered by the University of Chicago a course of study entirely on fellowship to take a Doctorate in Divinity, and they withdrew it when I wasn't willing to convert. I was then a teacher in California and was approached by the dean of the Divinity School who felt I had a religious vocation and asked if I would come to the University of Chicago and study with him. I said I would be delighted to do that but I would want the endpoint of that work to simply be a degree in Philosophy or a degree in Divinity, but I could not see myself ever converting. I said I would be tickled to death to preach, I would be tickled to death to preach to anyone, but under no specific instructions to speak for any specific faith.

Q: A Jewish priest! That would have been something!
A: You see, Mario, I was so mad, so quite berserk about these matters, that I saw no impediment to this, I saw no reason why I could not be a priest and still be a Jew, I saw no reason why I could not do this! It seemed to me altogether plausible. I felt that for them to seek conversion of me would be to violate my own sense of my own religiosity and my own spirituality. I am what I am and I know what I am, and that's it.

Q: Of course, it is inherent in Christianity to try to change people.
A: It was a most instructive occasion for me. It was terribly wounding, and the only two woundings on that score that I can report to you that had such power was that one, because they had romanced me for about a year, and they kept coming out to California and they would speak with me and say, "Oh, you would make a dandy fellow as a cleric." And then when they deprived me of going forward because I wouldn't yield. I was most, most distressed. And then again, you see, because I had so many children and I had such a paltry income, I sought at my students' suggestion to teach Sunday school at a synagogue, and when I went to see the rabbi there to see if I would be hired for the occasion, he said to me, "I understand that your wife is not Jewish. Is that correct, Mr. Lish?" And I said, "No, no, she's

not Jewish." "Well, I don't think we can have you teaching here." And I said, "Why not?" And he said, "Well, you would set a very, very poor example for the children." And I said, "You know, I regard your statement as entirely hostile to everything I understand about Judaism, and regard you as a despicable human being," and walked out. I was in a great huff. But you see, this is my general take on the official Jewish position as well. That rabbi who interviewed me, whose enthusiasm—at least for the discourse—was so considerable, as he claimed, and the program, which was called "The Eternal Light," eventually conspired not to hear my little truth. They wanted to shut it down. So that I have yet to find in normative Judaism any kind of welcome for dissent, any kind of welcome for the outlaw. No, they are entirely as ridden by fealty to a totalitarian position as any other faith would be.

I put before you, instead, the kind of apostasy that is practiced by Harold Bloom, who is no more, I suppose, religiously Jewish than am I, but in my regard is much more divinely inspired as a Jew than anyone I have ever known. Now I know Cynthia will have a conniption fit when she hears me say this, because I believe she sees Harold as, if not quite the devil, close to! But I see him as endowed with the most richly generous spirit of any thinker of that kind that I know, and I regard that as peculiarly Jewish.

Q: Well, just this morning Cynthia was telling me what a great thinker Harold Bloom is. This much she is able to recognize!
A: Of course she does, of course she does. Cynthia is surpassingly brilliant, as you must know, and she is the most dear of human beings. Her spaciousness of heart is without equal, and she would be the first to proclaim Harold Bloom's genius. But she would also, I think—

This interview, of which only the initial part is published here, took place in New York on January 23, 1990. It was conducted at Gordon Lish's favorite café near his office at Knopf. At the time of the interview, the rift between Lish and Harold Bloom had not yet taken place.

Interview with Gordon Lish

Patricia Lear / 1990

From *The American Story: The Best of StoryQuarterly* (New York: Cane Hill Press, 1990), pp. 241–51. © 1990 Patricia Lear. Reprinted by permission.

When he is teaching, Gordon Lish says he feels most himself. I watched him lecture in his fabled writers' workshop in New York City and he seemed to me to be possessed by the urgency of one who is constantly amazed. His spontaneity is the kind usually reserved for small children. We've got to listen! Feelings flow through him as if he were simply their conduit for six hours nonstop. There is no formula, no code. He discovers it as he goes along, and from moment to moment it is all new. His teaching is the result of a clear gift.

I attended two of the workshops in New York City in April 1987, and taped an interview in his office at Alfred A. Knopf where he is a senior editor. He also edits the new journal The Quarterly *and is the author of two novels,* Dear Mr. Capote, Peru, *and a story collection,* What I Know So Far. *Teaching is a role he has never spoken to, and although he agreed to the interview, when the interview was complete and the tapes in transcript form, he read them and felt that he did not, and cannot, and should not, speak to what goes on in the classroom. Having been present for what he does, and having read the creditable transcript of a creditable interview, I must admit that for him to reduce it to words is to reduce it, and that Gordon Lish the teacher is not made for the textbook, but rather for experience.*

Patricia Lear: I was afraid to meet you. I was afraid to interview you.
Gordon Lish: I can't imagine why. I'm a very mild fellow (laughs).

PL: Well, from what people have said about you. Many, many stories circulate. And last night, I was amazed at the love you put out. That's what struck me first. The intensity that you want this to work and the caring about these people, the writers in the room. I didn't expect that. I thought it would be the kind of thing where your students had to "earn" you. An uphill battle.

GL: Well, I expect that, not unlike any extraordinary event, if I may characterize what goes on in that room as an extraordinary event, those who are not present for it are inclined to develop rather inaccurate notions of what goes on. One has to be there. Much of the report that has centered on my private workshops is terrifically wide of the mark and not infrequently, I suppose, informed by a degree of presumption that arises out of displeasure. Displeasure because something's going on and one's not there for it, so it really can't be worth being there for. I don't think there's any way to quite capture the arc and character of one of those workshops without being present.

PL: Or you. Gordon Lish. I read a lot about you. Amy Hempel has told me about you. In my life all of a sudden you seem to be everywhere and you're not at all what I expected. I didn't even know when I walked into the workshop last night that was you and I've seen pictures of you. You're that different.

GL: Perhaps I've put on weight. Yes, that's probably it (laughs).

PL: But what I saw was a very open man, even somewhat vulnerable in his openness. Very genuine and real.

GL: You're very kind. But it may all be the teacher's device. One doesn't know. It may all be an act. I don't know what I do when I'm teaching. I really become, I think, transported in a kind of way and can't claim to be that person when I'm outside of a classroom setting. In a classroom setting, I have no fear and no hesitation and no doubt.

PL: So, at cocktail parties, you're not like that.
GL: No. Not at all.

PL: Have you always taught?
GL: I've taught since 1960. I was fired out of school-teaching. In, I guess it was, 1962, 1963, in California, and received the event with great ill will. I wanted to teach. I held teaching to be the highest calling.

PL: Was it high school or college?
GL: High school and junior college. I had gone from having the most lauding reports from my supervisors, to being cashiered for what I think eventually reduced itself to a case of rate-busting.

PL: Rape? Rate?
GL: Rate-busting is an expression that had favor with, ah, really disfavor, with trade unionists some years ago. Someone came along and turned out more widgets per hour than you were turning out—you went to your foreman and you delivered a complaint of rate-busting. Everybody had to turn out so many widgets—so if you were teaching, and then stayed on after school to keep teaching, you'd be likely to inspire a certain disapproval among your colleagues. So that what originally was a novelty, and much admired, and spoken of with enthusiasm by the administrators in that school district, after about three years, wasn't viewed with such pleasure by them at all. There was a lot of pressure on them to get rid of me. That in combination with my connections with people like Ken Kesey and Neal Cassady sent me packing in due course.

PL: Were they in the same place?
GL: Well, no. I was in a small town in California and they were in another small town in California, but we were loud enough to be heard. Kesey was a participant in my magazine, *Genesis West,* and we were all three great good pals.

PL: Were you writing then?
GL: No. I had abandoned writing some years before on the well-founded judgment that I would never be first-rate and that if you couldn't be first-rate, don't do it. I've since come to the view that everyone can be first-rate given an utter investment of will. But I had no will at that time. I would look across the way at writers like Stanley Elkin and Grace Paley and Edward Loomis and James Purdy and be convinced that what was present in their programs was something that would always be denied me. And so I was only too delighted to give up the task. I had, in my early twenties, even in my late teens I think it may have been, had two books accepted for publication here in New York. Both were really the kind of obvious undertakings of someone who has been in a nuthouse; you want quickly to report on the experience; partly, I think, to claim some points for yourself as having had the experience and partly to . . .

PL: Had you had that experience?
GL: Yes. Twice. And partly, too, I think to punish those persons you feel were responsible for it. So I had written two such novels. Both of them were wretched but not unremarkably wretched. Both were taken for publication and I therefore withdrew them. Not out of any kind of high standard that

suddenly occurred to me, but rather because I was fearful of disgracing my family. I withdrew both books—in one case, in galleys; paid back the money and that was that. Soon after, I took up the short story as an occupation. But that lasted not very long.

PL: You were around twenty-five now?
GL: Twenty-three, twenty-four, twenty-five, twenty-six; in there, I guess. I had a story that went out to the *Partisan Review*, a story whose title I will never forget. It was "Gasserpod, Gasserpod," which was a child's corruption of the word gastropod, I think it was. The *Partisan Review* held the story for an exceptionally long time. It may have been as long as two years, never responding to my letters. There must have been somewhere along the way that they gave me to believe that they were really, in fact, in possession of the story. Then, at the end of about three years, I got a letter from them rejecting the story (great laughter). I felt so keenly wounded by that experience I did not try to write fiction again, of a kind that I would put my name to. I had, in fact, written fiction all through the years that I was at *Esquire*. I would write under other names.

PL: Was that for any reason?
GL: To put chicken and peas on the table. I had four kids and *Esquire*'s wages to me were of such . . .

PL: They didn't want you moonlighting?
GL: They didn't really know about this, but I don't think they would have interfered. I've always been someone who worked around the clock. I never deprived *Esquire* of any of my energies. I would arrive for work at seven in the morning and work until at least eight at night. In fact, we not infrequently were there until twelve midnight. It was a highly keen bunch of folks. We were all quite enthusiastic about it. No few of us still remember it as the best time of our lives, when we were engaged on the *Esquire* that was Harold Hayes' *Esquire*. It's become many different *Esquire*s since.

PL: You were fired?
GL: By Clay Felker.

PL: No, no; before that. Out of California. How did you end up at *Esquire*?
GL: Well, I was fired out of school-teaching, and was told I should go teach in university and I'd say that isn't what I want to do; that what I

wanted to teach was high school, and I wanted to teach in the school my kids were going to be going to, and I wanted to live in the town I was living in then. And I sort of refused to take a university job. But I was around a lot of university people, and was working on a book on English syntax. I had a contract for two books on English grammar. I was putting out a literary magazine called *Genesis West*. It was being printed at a plant just south of San Francisco, and the man who headed up that plant said that he was printing a lot of material from an outfit called, I think it was, Sullivan Associates. And he thought this man, Sullivan, Maurice W. Sullivan, was the smartest man in the world. A man with two PhDs, three MAs, all that stuff, and he was much interested in the syntax of the language. The fellow thought I ought to get in touch with this Sullivan, that he and I would have common concerns and might hit it off, and I did. It was through Sullivan that I met a man who had been sort of Sullivan's teacher, or associate, and who headed up an outfit called the Behavioral Research Laboratories. At all events, BRL offered me a place to work and called me the Director of Linguistic Studies.

PL: What is Behavioral Research Laboratories?
GL: A high-sounding name for a rather straightforward affair. It was a clutch of behavioral psychologists and me, who is not a behavioral psychologist, putting together the means to teach people more efficiently, more effectively, than anybody could teach them in the absence of such means—from telling time and tying shoelaces to taking apart a rather abstruse sentence in English. So that's what I was doing there. And it was in that period that I went from teaching to developing teaching mechanisms and I began to do some work for the government, and put together, for the Office of Economic Opportunity, something called *A Man's Work*, and then another something called *Why Work?* And these things gave me some fame as someone who knew how teaching could be done, how learning could take place. And that all was abruptly set aside when I left California and took the *Esquire* job. I took the *Esquire* job, thinking that I would not last very long at it because it meant being in New York, which I'd left many years earlier. I used to be a radio actor here and I'd left because I thought New York had become uninhabitable.

PL: Were you brought in as fiction editor?
GL: Brought in as fiction editor, took over from Rust Hills, had to process manuscripts at a terrific clip.

PL: How do you do that?
GL: You just do it. Well, I don't want to tell anybody how I do it. Let them assume I don't read, okay, I don't read. I just take them out of their envelopes, and put them in other envelopes. Well, say I'm a reliable looker, not a reader, but a reliable looker. And I find what I'm looking for. I cannot go easy to my bed at night knowing that the day's work has not been surmounted. So that I simply will stay at it and stay at it and stay at it, looking and looking until the day's looking is done.

PL: You have four fulltime jobs. You're editing this new magazine, *The Quarterly*—
GL: Yes.

PL:—you're teaching, an editor here at Knopf and . . .
GL: And I write.

PL: How do you shift gears?
GL: I'm not so sure that that's really required because these activities tend to be continuous with one another. Certainly my editing and my teaching seem to me to draw on the same impulse. The only occasion requiring me to reset myself is when I come to the page as a writer. And that's because there's a certain arrogance in teaching and editing. However much one doesn't want to be, one is forced to make judgments of a kind that tend to objectify questions. Whereas the kinds of judgments one makes as a writer oughtn't to be all that objective. And I'm very inclined to be rather too clinical as a writer, rather too knowing in my approach to the text; rather too observing and too conscious of what the values are; what the structure is; how it might be made another. I know too much, is what I'm trying to say, and I'm inclined to believe it's desirable not to know so much. I'm inclined to become too clever on the page so that I end up speaking only to a certain form of attention in myself rather than to my whole heart. My short stories tend to be too intricate, too shrewd.

PL: That's it. I've read your stories and I expected you to be very different than you are.
GL: Yes. They tend to be very self-reflexive and . . .

PL: To me, you're not like your work.
GL: But, contrastively, my novels, the ones, the two that I've signed my name to, I've written fifteen, twenty books under other names, when I was

at *Esquire,* and made large sums of money from doing so; novels and nonfiction. The two novels I put my name to, and the one I'm working on now, represent different versions of myself. Come out of a deeper place in me. They are all as fraudulent because they arise out of some kind of exercise I do with myself. So they're also fraudulent; I'm of the opinion that in uncovering ourselves we simply set aside one fraudulence for another. But at the moment that we reveal the new layer beneath, I'm sure we're earnestly convinced that we've touched the bone, revealed something authentic. But there is nothing authentic. It's just theater. Us the audience for ourselves or God the audience.

PL: Could you go over last night, what you were saying about the role of art and its importance? In your class you set such standards; you speak of art in a way that I've never heard.
GL: Art is a way to manage our death. I think we die more easily, or less horribly, to the extent that we have done our work. The crudest being is competent to summon for himself some kind of magic for managing his mortality. A bean, a pebble, he's got a magic pebble in his pocket. Even if it's only the pressure of his grasp on the hand of a friend that is sitting at his bedside. We, all of us, I think, require magic to manage life. That's what art is—magic. What I try to do is relieve my students of the notion that they can't stick out; to convince them that everything that is required for sticking out is present in them.

PL: So you screen them for will.
GL: Absolutely.

PL: How do they apply?
GL: No formal process. It's often by recommendation. Somebody else, they know someone . . .

PL: What if someone is reading this and says, Oh I want to do this workshop? I get it. They have to find their own way.
GL: They have to find a way. They have to come find me (laughter). I'll give you an example of what will happen. Someone will call me up, say, "Gee, I read about your workshop, and I'd like to know if it would be possible to get in it." And I say, "Well, let's talk about that." And at the end of the conversation, I'll say, "Well, now I think it would be wise to sum up these remarks in a letter to me." So then they say, "Oh. Oh. You want a letter." And I say, "Yes, yes, I want a letter," and they'll say, "Well, where are you?" and

I'll say, "Alfred Knopf," and they'll say, "Well, what's the address there? "The address?" I say. "You want the address?"

PL: Just figure it out.
GL: Figure it out. Because, you see, it's not for whimsy, nor for caprice, that I take this position. I know if they don't have the kind of resolve to persevere in the face of *that* small task, how in the world will they *ever ever ever* stand up to . . .

PL: To what happens next.
GL: To what happens next, exactly.

PL: Do you look at manuscripts at all?
GL: Oh, sure. But I don't take any of the writing that is put to me as a sample of ability quite as seriously as I do the person himself.

PL: When you talk about the lengths people go to, to be admitted, and then what they have to deal with in their lives to get here—you've had people move here, and take apartments . . .
GL: It's an enormous, enormous investment. I just had a fellow who wanted to move here for the term from Paris.

PL: Have you grown over the years?
GL: Every time I teach a class I am instructed by what is put on the table as much as is anybody in the class. Every time anybody else comes away with a deal of knowing, I come away with a deal of knowing, too. I have no hesitation to talk about other aspects of my life, but I've never really talked about my teaching. I used to let people record it because I would feel that (1) there ought to be a record and (2) if persons who were legitimate participants could not be present for a certain class, the tape could then be sent to them or be available to them. And I stopped doing that . . .

PL: But why?
GL: Because even the tape, out of the context of the class, seemed an eerie and inaccurate object.

Gordon Lish

Alexander Neubauer / 1994

From *Conversations on Writing Fiction: Interviews with Thirteen Distinguished Teachers of Fiction Writing in America* (New York: Harper, 1994), pp.154–75. © 1994 Alexander Neubauer. Reprinted by permission.

Gordon Lish, while still in his teens, had a career as a radio broadcaster, actor, and disc jockey. As an editor at Alfred A. Knopf (since 1977) and of the literary magazine *The Quarterly*; as the author of five novels (including *Dear Mr. Capote*, 1983), three collections of short fictions, and many essays and edited anthologies; and as a teacher of one of the most well-known independent writing classes in the country, his name today is recognized on three fronts. His activities in and around teaching, especially, have been the subject of scores of newspaper and magazine articles, many quite recent.

Still, writers, editors, teachers, and students of writing who may know his name or have heard of marathon seven-hour classes may know much less of his actual teaching methods and theories underlying them. In the following conversation, Gordon Lish discusses an array of subjects, among them the immortality of art, the seduction of the reader, the composition of sentences, and the ardor needed for a writing life, his own and his students'. "The only way one can keep on," he says here, "as Picasso kept on, as Degas kept on, as no few artists do keep on . . . in the face of every kind of reason to succumb, is to find in the will, in desire, a superior response."

Gordon Lish has taught at Yale, Columbia, and New York universities. His most recent works are the novel *Zimzum* (1993) and *Ten Bits* (1993), a collection of short fiction. In the spring of 1993 he was awarded an honorary doctor of letters degree from the State University of New York.

This conversation took place in New York City, which is the site of his independent classes.

Alexander Neubauer: Let me begin by asking you how the students in your classes are selected.
Gordon Lish: Well, almost entirely on the basis of will. Desire. If I have one place left, and there is a student who will fly in from Portland, Oregon, a student who will move to New York for three months, a student who will commute back and forth to Chicago, as against a student who will roll out of bed and take the bus across town, I'm likely to take the one who will undertake the greater inconvenience. I'm willing to believe that everything depends upon ardor, on will, on desire, on resolve. And if the student can demonstrate that resolve by his statements, by his acts, as against the student who fancies himself very gifted, very talented, I'm going to bet on the hungrier rat.

Q: What does "will" mean, in the context of writing?
A: Will is everything. Desire is everything. In this activity and in life. One must want, and want so greatly, that every sort of impediment is only another occasion for the determination of the student to seek its solution, and in such solutions finding new prospects for problems further on. Everything wants your failure. The body that you inhabit, the time that is yours, the circumstances of your life, every particularity that can be summoned to the general spectacle of your enterprise through space and time, can be seen as an interference to doing great art—nothing more efficiently than the mortality that is your due. And to exert ceaselessly in the face of such circumstances is to require an exorbitant desire. One must want so greatly that every reason to succumb is dismissed.

As one goes forward making the composition, one is always establishing a move, a gesture, a decision, an election that defeats what has been offered up by the composition itself. One is engaged in a kind of global and rapid-fire problem-solving procedure that might be seen as offering moves against moves. For every move that is made, there is a countermove.

Well, likewise, as the composition is done, so is done the life which encompasses the artist. One is certain to be continually offered up by experience reasons to quit, reasons to turn back and start anew. One will be shown why one is insufficient, incompetent to proceed. And in order to proceed, one must continually mount solutions—resolutions in the case of living one's life—against those impediments. One has to *earn* one's life as an artist.

In my own life now, for example, I am confronted with enormous personal difficulties in the context of my family, my getting income and the like. Everyone who does life, as against resigning from life, will be constantly caught up in contest with an array of impediments. Eventually we are all entirely surrounded by circumstances which want our defeat and which invade ever more persuasively toward that end. As one ages, one is certain to find that the body is increasingly going to announce its villainy. The only way one can keep on—as Picasso kept on, as Degas kept on, as no few artists do keep on, as Stephen Hawking, the cosmologist, kept on and kept on in the face of every kind of reason to succumb, is to find in the will, in desire, a superior response.

Q: But aren't you also assuming a level of artistic talent on the part of the writer?
A: No, no, I don't see a connection. And as a matter of fact in my own instruction as a teacher of writing—although my concerns are specifically the production of prose fiction, the enabling of my students to produce literary artifacts of a kind that invite the attention of history—I nevertheless feel required to oblige them to consider the totality of the problem that confronts them. It is not enough to be adroit at the composition of sentences; one must be adroit at living a life in the face of the prospects of defeat. I know so many young persons—no, I know so many *persons*—marvelously endowed, who are so deprived of an effective reckoning with the life problem that they have either abandoned the activity or let the activity decline and decline, to the point where it is at a great remove from history's concerns.

So that I don't think that talent or gift, if such things do exist, have anything to do with what the final receipts will be. My notion is that anyone who speaks, by reason of that speech, has the prospect of achieving important imaginative writing. I see the notion of talent as quite irrelevant. I see instead old-fashioned notions of perseverance, application, industry, assiduity, *will, will, will, desire, desire, desire.*

Q: Ninety-nine percent perspiration, one percent inspiration?
A: Absolutely, absolutely. And I think it is not at all difficult to state the matter that simply. Everything is will and the great obstacle is always fear. It comes down in every instance to this dualism between what one wants and what one may be afraid to have.

Q: Before asking you about the actual method of composition you teach, I'd like to touch briefly on the question of academic writing programs.
A: Well, I can't really claim to be informed. I have very slight knowledge of what in fact obtains in the formal programs where one matriculates for a master of fine arts, until there are even some schools now that offer doctoral degrees in imaginative writing. Absurd on the face of it. But there may be in

fact profit for people who pursue such degrees. I can only speak to my own program, which of course as you know is entirely without any kind of formal procedures and lacks certainly the formal evidence that is present in a university setting. I can't give a degree and I can't give a certificate. I can only offer my own exertions in the matter, which tend to be—I understand from those who have experienced both the formal setting and my own—rather exorbitant.

Q: You taught at Yale.
A: I taught at Yale, Columbia, at NYU, and I don't think whatever criticism I might want to assign to those settings is necessarily the fault of the setting itself or the setting itself susceptible to some kind of defect. People are people, they do what they will do in whatever setting you put them in. Certainly such observation is as appropriate for students as it is for teachers. Students who come to me, recognizing that they cannot at the end of their time with me point to a document which presumably entitles them to conduct professional activities of either a teaching or a writing kind, I think may demonstrate considerably more will and desire and *courage* than those who come away from the experience with a piece of paper in their hand. It may be that the very character of my classes in respect to what you *cannot* get from them creates a self-sorting process that delivers to me animated students.

Q: And as far as actual composition is concerned—if one could separate craft, style, language on the one hand, and content on the other, you have a strong view about the first part, the way sentences should be put together in writing. One of your students described your method as "walking backwards."
A: Yes.

Q: Unlike traditional narrative fiction.
A: My argument is that one can arrive at an enormously *more* effective artifact, that is, a storytelling act, if one is attendant upon a procedure called *recursion,* which means that in essence one finds one's utterance by reason of one's examination of what has *already* been uttered. The utterance that you are at this point embarking on takes its origin from what has just been stated prior to it. Traditional storytelling, or the art of storytelling, is rather more recursive than discursive, though I recognize there's not always a sharp line between them.

There's much more to this than what I've just stated because one requires additionally the notion of *torque,* or what I sometimes call "the swerve," in order to bring about the arcs of the story. So that on the one hand one finds the origins for one's current utterance in what is prior, but one is always in a combative relation with what is prior. And this combat, this torque, must issue forth sentence by sentence by sentence or utterance by utterance by utterance. One can construe the parts of the composition as sentences if one wishes, or as paragraphs, or as other kinds of units, entirely depending on the steepness of the arc one is in search of.

I think, to put it as plainly as I might, the answers arrive out of examining what is prior and swerving from it. It is rather like the generation of a plant issuing from itself. At one point there was nothing there, and the singularity which set everything in motion from the seed, like the original singularity of the cosmos, contains within it the potential for everything that might issue forth: sentences, paragraphs, chapters, pages. Everything is dependent or contingent on what is prior. This arrangement of contingencies is in fact the narrative act. I'm giving it to you in the most simple-minded fashion, because there are sophistications in this procedure which could keep us seated here in exchange for months without having touched the right ones.

Q: One wouldn't, putting it even more simply, know the plot before one started—one wouldn't have it worked out?
A: There is no plot. Plot is not a dishonorable concept. [But] we are talking here of the production of the kind of writing that stands the greatest chance of moving literary art forward on the great historical wheel of the national literature. We are not talking about creating product in the marketplace; we are not talking about getting published; we are not talking about anything other than how to come into possession of a totality, an utter totality, which seizes the attention of the best readers of your time.

I would want, since this is my time, to be read by Harold Bloom and Denis Donoghue and Julia Kristeva and a couple of dozen other persons whose names I could recite for you. And that would really be the only thing I would want. If I could seduce their attention into a rapture that I like to assign as "the gaze," I would feel I had done ably in enacting my art. I don't know very many better readers than Denis Donoghue or Harold Bloom or Don DeLillo or Cynthia Ozick. If I could manage to mount a succession of events that enforce "the gaze" in any of the persons just named, I would feel accomplished and pleased with my efforts and see them as having brought about the end that I wish for them, and that's all that I wish. The event of publication, the event of reviewing, all the rest of that fame, notice, is beyond the realm of my concern.

Q: So when you said earlier that you want to enable students to "invite the attention of history," what you mean is . . . ?
A: One can undertake every sort of recreative act in a hobbyist kind of way; one can go run around the park in the expectation that one is going to keep his body furnished against the tide of time, but one knows that that is not possible to do. But in art, one likes to think, one is not subject necessarily to the incommensurate power of time. There are ways, I do think, to exert force, perhaps even commensurate force, against the exigencies of time and space. And it seems to me that the only reason to undertake an activity of such an entirely difficult kind is for the sake of history.

It must be very hard to run around in the park, you know, so many miles every day. It must be very hard; I've never tried it—I imagine it would be an unthinkable act to me, I couldn't run around the block—but those persons who can do this, say, who can run a marathon, must be persons of extraordinary zeal and absolutely majestic resolve. I would answer, "For what?" In the end they are defeated. We're reduced to, in any event, simply drawing fictions against reality. I mean, all Stephen Hawking is doing as he comes into possession of some kind of cosmological structure is seeking to project a fiction that is continuous with his mind, and which reclaims his lost hegemony over reality. One is seeking, in the doing of prose fiction, the same kind of reclamation of hegemony over reality. One enters into a certain kind of concentration and projects a fiction, presumably, desirably, powerful enough to penetrate time and space. To undertake such a remarkable act for anything other than heroic reasons seems to me pointless. History is the only arena.

Q: Let me go back to the subject of composition, sentences and so forth . . .
A: Well, composition is really the only lie. The assembly of this succession of utterances is a lie. It is achieved by reason of an array of decisions that have nothing to do with what we would like to think of as the probity, the honesty, in the occasion. That is to say, the work is set in motion, by reasons of one's embrace of a right object. An entirely outrageous literary performer will prove to be reckless enough to embrace among his right objects the object that, at that moment in his experience, is his *rightest* object. Such an object is unique to himself and dangerously engaged. But that's the end of it. Once I have accomplished that reckless act into which one rushes forth by reason of one's audacity, that's an end of the irrational—and therefore the honest. All of that craft, all of that art, is empty of truth. It has as its teleology only the achievement of "the gaze" in the reader, at the expense of every other concern. The assembly, the composition, is a lie, from beginning to end.

Q: A willing lie, a knowing lie?

A: One is an idiot, one is a fool, one is a naïf if one thinks otherwise. Doing great literary composition is an act for grown-ups, not for children, and one can perform these acts importantly only when one is entirely alert to every nuance of what is at issue in the making of composition. And one must be responsive. You're playing a game. Remember, I gave you the theme for this earlier. I said, there's a move for every move. Well, in fact, as you go forward in an act of composition, as you accrue sentences, accrue utterances, that theme becomes infinitely complex. There are an infinite number of moves for every number of moves. The artifact that you are struggling to achieve answers you at every unitary step with a widening array of moves. And you have therefore to find ever more complex solutions. So as the lie exfoliates, it becomes compounded exponentially and takes you farther and farther from anything that might be claimed to be honest, true. And this is a procedure of such startling difficulty that it could scarcely be accomplished with any deftness by someone who is unalert to what he was doing.

Q: And the result, I'm quoting some from you and your students, is writing that "sticks to the page"?

A: Well, someone may have produced a sentence which I regard as very breathy, not a voiced sentence, one in which there's a high incidence of unvoiced syllables, and I might say, "It's not really clamped to the page. It doesn't stick to the page." But that doesn't help us very much, does it? You have to first know what it is to produce a sentence that has in it a great deal of acoustical pressure.

Q: Would you say, though, that there is a sound, a language quality among your writers?

A: No, no, no. There can never be. Well, I think I've heard it observed by impresarios who have arranged for my students to read somewhere that their prose seems remarkably spoken, remarkably musical, that the distinction between the writing my students and other persons perform was extraordinary. That there is a much more vocal and forceful effect delivered.

I can tell you why this is the case: A great deal of time is spent in my classes bearing in on what it is to create an acoustical event and how one parses out the properties of utterances. One then understands how they are to be manipulated in order to heighten the acoustical character of the sentence. My students become, if they're able, very deft at crafting sentences so that sensory effects of the most subtle kind are within their dominion.

You see, the task is really reducible to a few very plain statements. As I've said, there is a move for every move, and in recursive composition the moves one needs to consider exfoliate exponentially against the array of moves one can make as responses. One can also say that the prize goes to him who can control everything. We are talking essentially about an act whose success reposes entirely in the matter of control. Now, if I say to you, "Your job is to control everything that you have produced to the attention of the reader, to be in control, or to use Coleridge's expression, that you have "invested your voice, your authority, in every phrase you have set down on the page," well then the question becomes: What is that "everything"? How much do you see? Are you concerned to know the sentence as a grammatic act, are you concerned to know the sentence as a syntactic act, how many ways can you begin to see what is present or potentially present in the office of the sentence? The more you know about the potentialities of sentences, the wider or bigger that "everything" is going to be for you.

Well, my job as a teacher, it seems to me, is to widen and widen my students' apprehension of what that "everything" is, and then give them the means by which to exert control over it. Now, obviously, I cannot enumerate all the conditions that will confront them as they do composition. If they're doing composition in the right kind of ways, conditions will be novel. And the solutions that will be adduced to their reckoning will have to be novel as well. But what I *can* do is to habituate them in the art of seeing and acting. I can establish their vision of what the composition is, and I can sharpen their possession of themselves as persons able to arrive at solutions for every potentiality. In the end the greatest artifact will be produced by that writer who has had the most global control over his material. It therefore follows that I have to achieve in my students—since I want in them nothing less than the first prize—the powers of perception and of determination. That "everything" is in the vision of Dawn Raffel clearly larger than in the vision of her inferior. She sees more.

DeLillo and I say, when we chat in the little that we ever do about difficulties we are both confronting in our own work, that the more obdurate the wall one is facing, the more glorious will be the window one is able to produce in that wall, and the more fabulous will be the vista that one will then see. So one is always seeking.

I mean, it's all about how much you can possibly see, and how resolute you will be in seeking your answer to what is seen. Nothing is ceded; nothing is yielded. The story owns none of itself. You own it all. There is no story apart from your intervention; there never was. I'm told that Saul

Bellow was once asked what Augie March would have to say in reflection on Reaganomics. My own reply, were I asked to sit as Bellow's coach on the matter, would have been: Tell them there is no Augie March. Tell them he is occasions of ink on a sheet of paper, and the personality they have come to imagine is a function of the arrangement of those occasions of ink on the sheet of paper. You have successfully achieved the projection of a fiction such that it penetrates time and space, and you've made believers, and they are fools, fools. The reader is present to the artifact only such that his seduction might be sought. One wants from him nothing more than his rapture.

You see, quite wonderfully, the greatest readers are also those who are most enraptured, should the artifact have the competency to prove that response in them. I recently read against my will Cormac McCarthy's *Blood Meridian*, and was enraptured, thoroughly his creature, so that even in the face of what I took to be McCarthy's failures of judgement, I was helplessly his creature. I cannot point to very many objects and artifacts of that kind in my recent life. It thoroughly seduced me despite every effort I had to resist it. I would regard it as a work of art of nothing less than surpassing power.

Q: In terms of the material from which students draw forth their writing, you ask for a good deal of truth-seeking.
A: Well, my position is entirely this: If great art were a function of great erudition, there'd be very little for those of us who claim to be teachers to do. My own feeling is, as I remarked earlier, that the power of speech is ample for one's making the most heroic beginning so long as this power is wedded to equal possession of one's self, one's will, one's desire. The only source from which one can hope to achieve the seduction of history is what reposes in the self. This has nothing to do with education, nothing to do with erudition, nothing to do with reading the encyclopedia.

I ask my students to enter upon an examination of themselves in order to find those objects in themselves which have the greatest potency, a potency, should it be manipulated in a public setting, [that] might produce danger to their lives. By manipulating it in a public setting, they make themselves susceptible to every kind of harm; and this is where we begin. It is a psychoanalytic act which has in it no therapist. One is always in pursuit of tropes—symbols seen as objects which stand for other objects—and hoping to annihilate them by the act of writing, finding in fact what they were an evasion of—other tropes—and so on and so. And you are always many tropes behind yourself. But that's OK. Meanwhile you get an art out of it until you've worn yourself out. These are your materials.

Now I don't mean, in any of this, that one is in search of the abstract. On the contrary. For example, one's sense of mortality would never be acceptable as an object, but one's father's wristwatch might be, you see.

I give them to understand the shaman or the witch doctor, who presents himself to those foregathered for him. The witch doctor empties from the pouch he carries on his belt a piece of wing bone, a piece of shell, a pebble, a stick. It's like that. Now, what would be your pebble, your piece of broken bone? We all of us have a pocket, many pockets. I'm asking you to take out of your pocket those objects you're earnestly possessed of. And I'm not interested in students who promote fiction to begin with. I'm interested in the students who have the courage to actually empty out their handbags onto the table and say, "Well, you know I've got this battery here, I've a nine-volt battery." It's very different than saying, "I'm enraged with my husband; I don't like my husband because he's too short." No, "I have a nine-volt battery." The first sentence might in fact say, "This battery is possessed of nine volts of power." And the second sentence might say, "Had I a battery possessed of any fewer volts of power, it would be insufficient to do the job that this battery does." And so on. One would begin to weave his sentences, his utterances, in such recursive style until eventually perhaps engaging even *the meaning* of that nine-volt battery.

But I'm not interested in meaning. I seek in my students an appreciation for dearth of meaning. I'm interested in the seduction of the reader. Meaning is irrelevant. I am not interested in compositions which seek to uncover mysteries; I'm interested in compositions which seek to propose mysteries. A great writer need not be smart, he need only be clever. The witch doctor wants to continue on as the witch doctor; he wants to be assigned that role in the tribe the following season. That's all he wants, his continued hegemony over the tribe.

Q: In your observation of the learning curves of your students, as they work with sentences on the one hand, themselves on the other hand . . .
A: Which happens faster?

Q: Which happens faster and which kinds of students are able to do one and not the other?
A: Yes, very good question. You've asked me a question no one's ever asked me before. I can probably say with some vehemence—seeing my students through the other end of a telescope—that those who go on to have careers expressive of astonishing strengths of craft interest me much less than those

who prove to have astonishing possession of themselves, of their evasions. It's lovely when one finds the wedding of the two, and then one has such a person as Dawn Raffel or Victoria Redel or Christine Schutt in my current class. Ben Marcus is a fellow who has colossal possession of the manipulations but probably rather less possession of his "objects"—or is launched, let us say, on a less audacious discovery of his objects. But of course Ben Marcus is twenty-four or twenty-five; Dawn Raffel must be thirty-five. So we are also speaking of abilities that have no little to do with where one is in life.

I will say something I feel required to say. I think in the main, my students, as they begin to make their way, are very inclined to drift from the more puzzling, the more arduous aspects of this activity, and to let it be filled up with easier objects. They find that their handiwork is so deft and at such a remove from those with whom they are competing that it's quite ample for them to make their way in the world. So that they do rather handily by simply being handy. Were I to have my way, I would prove able to build into them a more desperate relation to what I think is the moral work of being an artist.

At a certain part of my examinations of these matters I would have held Harold Brodkey aloft as easily our most interesting writer, and I continue to think that certain enterprises of his, in the collection *Stories in an Almost Classical Mode*, are far and away the best things in the language. We don't have anything better than certain of Brodkey's stories, which I take to be equal of the best novels we have. And I'm only satisfied with my students when they evince comparable relations to the moral work. When they fall from that difficult mark, then I am likely to be disappointed in them. Too many of my students let themselves be pried away from that moral work.

Q: While under your auspices.
A: No, afterward. No, under my auspices I think I rather keep them to the mark. I'm rather fussy about these things. I'm not easily pleased at all. And my students usually do want to please me.

It's hard to give you a picture of these classes. I mean, they're different in every instance—every class from every other class. For example, the classes I taught this summer were seven and a half hours long, and no one talked but myself. And it was a thoroughly enshrouding experience for all of us. It is not easy to be in such a setting and be unserious. You know, if you can sit seven hours without getting up to visit the facilities or to nibble at something, that's comparable to flying from New York to Vienna, for example, without getting up to relieve yourself. Well, my students do better than that, actually. So you would take them to be serious people, given to behaving in accordance with the most taxing material in the class, which is the moral material.

But once you are deprived of the office of such a setting [where] others are doing the same crazy thing and someone is hectoring you and hectoring you to meet some exorbitant mark all the time, once you return to the awful burden of your isolation, it may seem a lot more appealing to do a deft piece of composition than to begin a heroic piece of uncovering. So the moral work is the rather more perplexing of the two, and certain writers for whom I've had the highest hopes, the highest hopes, become diverted by the temptations of the marketplace.

Q: Which are ever-present?
A: Well, you see, I hope to impart to my students an indifference to the marketplace. Certainly you are right, the marketplace encroaches upon them as they begin to exhibit sufficient skill to get themselves in print; they are enticed away. They will publish with me, for example, an effective collection of stories, and the next thing you know someone has called up and wants to assign them the job of interviewing a bunch of Olympic swimmers, which has nothing to do with the art they have acquired. Certain ones of these persons will say, "No, I think not. This is not what I'm a writer for, it's not what I'm about." But others will be enchanted and distracted; they can now interview on assignment and the hell with sitting at home and writing fiction. I have seen this pattern quite a lot, and there will only be the few of them that will be able to resist such blandishment. Despite the strictness of my classes, despite the high order of the moral requirement, as it were, the bulk of them will very quickly be seduced away. It's a great sadness to me, a great sadness.

Not infrequently, I must also observe, once having let themselves be taken away, they find themselves wanting back in again and can't get back in again. It's impossible to ever forget the broad spacious grandness of the boulevards and the whiteness of the buildings. They just can't get back to their awful labors again.

To do composition in the terms I propose is to be solitary. That alone is more than they can bear. It means always to write against your time, it means to write outside your time, it means the instant you are claimed by official organisms to be a writer of a certain kind you are now obliged to move on to a new space. They don't want to do that. It's much easier to let themselves be typified and then work to a model that is successful in the marketplace. It's really the rare artist who is able to sustain an idea of himself as an artist, but this is true in every pursuit. It is scarcely more the case in the literary arts than it is in any other kind.

And indeed, in this respect, we can properly encompass within the definition of artist anyone, in any practice, who undertakes that which has not been done before. In this context, Stephen Hawking is as much as an artist as Albert Einstein was, as much an artist as Sigmund Freud was. Harold Bloom will continually insist these were our great poets. Sigmund Freud was a great poet; Karl Marx was a great poet. These are persons who projected great fictions onto the imagination of the world. That's what it is. But as history teaches us, it's a most discouraging labor, given that one, although he is working outside of time, is living in his time.

I have among my closest friends James D. Watson, who along with Francis Crick proposed the molecular structure of DNA. He and Crick worked in virtual isolation from the bulk of their fellows, single-mindedly engaged at a cost of the most exorbitant kind—reputation and the like. But what do they do lately? Have they been able to keep to such a mark over the course of their inventive lives, their intellectual lives? It's a lot easier to go to a party, a lot easier to be interviewed as I am letting myself be done now, than to be about my own solitary labors as a writer. It's easier to enact the pose in the context where one has one's audience than it is to do the work.

Q: One of your students told me that you considered teaching "a pure activity."
A: That's right. It's the purest thing I do.

Q: You think of yourself that way first, as a teacher?
A: *Yes.* I recognize in myself larger satisfactions from this activity than from all others that I've engaged in. Furthermore, I am able to achieve more honesty in this activity than in any of the others. When I'm in a classroom, for that allotted time, I am closer to the truth of myself than I am in any other activity of my life. Whether professional or otherwise. I am more of myself as a teacher than I am as a writer or as an editor or as a husband or as a father or as a friend. And I am as a teacher most alive to myself. So that I like myself in that context and find myself deriving from it more pleasure than I do in any other context. I come closer to getting myself shed of what I don't like about myself. And in fact, in this wise, teaching improves. Whereas contrastively, writing declines. I less and less like myself as a writer. I more and more see myself incompetent of escaping from my distractions.

Q: Your students know of your role as editor also. And in terms of *The Quarterly*, there's a potential at least for those you like to be published.
A: Yes, if I have taught someone to write ably I am not a little interested from profiting from that ability. It sometimes wounds me greatly when my students don't wish to have me publish them. They would sooner be published elsewhere. I find that sometimes very troublesome, very dismaying; I see it almost as a kind of disloyalty, but it happens a lot. Quite a lot. My students say, "Well, gee, Gordon, I'm very pleased you want that piece but I'd sooner publish it in another literary magazine," for whatever reasons are at hand.

Q: Few have turned down a book contract, though.
A: That's a different thing. I think that has happened. I try not to let it happen because I try to be there from the first. They are emerging writers and I'm the one who's first aware of that emergence, and so I try to seize these people before anybody else can get their hands on them. In fact, Anderson Ferrell represented a case of someone I seized with only one paragraph he'd written and I gave him a book contract based on that paragraph. It was a fine novel called *Where She Was*, and now he's engaged on writing a much finer novel, which I also have under contract.

But certainly if your question goes to the point that my students have an added cause of ardor in my case, given that I might act as an editor on their behalf . . . but then of course this really exists one way or another in no few writing classes, where the teacher may himself be under contract and tips off someone. One way or another I suppose it can be claimed that any student in any kind of formal setting anywhere, in a university or not in a university, is going to be in touch with somebody who has his hands in closer touch with the reins that can provide print.

Q: It may stir competition, but that may not necessarily be a bad thing?
A: But I'm all for competition. I can't get enough of it. I think that we are all of us, even in entirely isolated terms, engaged in a competition. Competition becomes the dynamic by which all growth takes place. It necessarily follows from the circumstance; one hardly has to inject it.

First of all, one necessarily seeks the approval of the teacher, the father, as is natural in the family romance. I am in that context the father. There is a person who is in authority and others who are seeking to have the approval of that authority. Even if I were to promote by words and deeds every air of cooperation, you can't empty the circumstance of that dynamic, nor would I want to.

I have taught creative writing for over thirty years. I have absolutely not the least doubt that those who prove best able to acquire the poetics that I'm promulgating are invariably those who are the most determined. And I've seen the other kind again and again. Highly verbal persons, they've been told their lives long that they should be writers, been told they've written beautifully and convince themselves they've written beautifully, who prove not to have the moral bearing, at least in the circumstance of my class. I tend to be very suspicious of those who think themselves very greatly talented. And I tell them, "What do you want to come to me for? If you think you're writing beautiful now, what do you think I can add to that?" "Well, everyone says you're great." I say, "But my greatness resides really in my getting rid of everything you think is beautiful." No. I'm much more inclined to want to bet on somebody who is approaching these matters humbly and who sees themselves as virtually deprived, but who for crazy reasons wants to be a writer.

Q: Has your teaching changed over the years?
A: Every set of classes change and change. I think there's been a decisive strengthening of my teaching since my personal difficulties have become so considerable, as I expect I'm finding the need to take my happiness, such as it can be taken, from my classes.

And I've seen life play itself out in certain ways that convince me that art is the only escape. When there is no escape, art is the only pretense that has any durability to it. Other pretenses are too quickly doomed. Religion is certainly a conventional and successful answer, and the only one I think that answers the one that art makes. I don't see flight, I don't see drugs, I don't see the life of unreason as a successful enough reply. One must make a reply or one succumbs to the reality principle and surrenders early on, one becomes the living dead. So one makes a reply in fiction or in art, and it occurs to me that *art,* this art, real art, at least has the virtue of sustaining itself rather longer in time and rather more widely in space than others. It seems to me, anyway.

Q: This is really a first question, but who were your teachers? You've spoken of Edward Loomis.
A: Yes, yes. I only had one formal writing teacher. It was at the University of Arizona, and it was Edward Loomis. I think I lasted two or three meetings. I remember running from his class in what must have been barely contained tears. I know that when I returned home I surely dissolved into hysterics

before my wife and children, feeling that I had been used badly by a bully, and of course the use he made of me was entirely for my own good and I was too little an artist to understand this. In subsequent years I came to be very disappointed in myself for not having proved to have the mettle to stand up to his extraordinary intellect and moral bearing.

So Loomis has had I think a not inconsiderable impact on my ideas of myself as a man first, and as a writer and teacher secondarily. I've learned more from his short story, "A Kansas Girl," about a life given over to service, to duty, to strictness, than I ever did in any writing class I had with him. Before that time, I found myself powerfully taught by Poe, Joyce, Beckett, Emily Dickinson, Whitman, Emerson. I claim to have the greatest affiliation with certain European and Latin American writers. I find myself really willing to declare I never finished a single book by Borges, but I'm much enamored of the idea of such an affiliation. I really can't claim to having ever read a word of *Ulysses,* nor would I want to, and yet I feel myself in certain ways the result of my *idea* of Joyce. I think Harold Bloom would claim that strong writers only read themselves, and that it is your misreading of your precursors that counts. So it is my misapprehension of Joyce, of Beckett. I can't deny that for three or four years of my life I virtually saw my walk as consonant with the walk I imagined James Joyce had. But I was probably more taught by Joyce's letters than I was by his prose fiction.

Today, every time I read DeLillo I learn from DeLillo, I learn from Brodkey, I learn from Ozick, I learn from any of the persons I admire. I probably can claim to learn the most from the last strong writer I read. So Cormac McCarthy has taught me the most.

Q: Just as you speak of your experience with Loomis, I would think perhaps there are some students who have not been prepared to profit from Gordon Lish.
A: Oh, I don't doubt there have been a lot of those! I think I have probably run off many more from my classes than Loomis has. I'm sure he's a much more tactful and gentle presence than anything I might claim to have been. I don't doubt that I have made many more enemies by reason of my teaching than I have made friends, and I really am willing, as painful as it is, to reckon with that as a citizen in the world. As a teacher I think I am probably achieved in this respect. I don't think any strong student should go away from a strong teacher feeling friendly to that teacher. I think he should be bent upon that teacher's undoing. Please God the student will have the grace and wisdom to know that the undoing should take place within the

context of doing prose fiction, not in sitting down and writing for a popular magazine a hatchet piece about his teacher. Not too many go away with that in mind. If they want to undo you, they call you at three o'clock in the morning and shriek into the telephone.

I don't doubt I've made a lot of unhappy persons in my classes. I can't say I'm sorry for that except insofar as it has abutted personal life. I don't like being made the object of assault in popular magazines. I do rather like a student who goes away determined to outwrite that son of a bitch eight ways to Sunday. That's swell, let him try.

Gordon Lish

Douglas Glover / 1995

Broadcast 1/23/1995. © *The Public Radio Book Show*, produced by Northeast Public Radio/ WAMC and the New York State Writers Institute. Reprinted by permission.

Douglas Glover: Welcome to *The Book Show*. I am your host, Douglas Glover. My guest today is the celebrated and flamboyant "Captain Fiction," aka Gordon Lish, author, editor, and teacher extraordinaire. He has been a fiction editor at *Esquire Magazine,* and, for eighteen years, at Alfred A. Knopf, from which he was recently fired. He has published such names as Raymond Carver, Barry Hannah, and Amy Hempel. As if that wasn't enough, he single-handedly publishes his own literary magazine *The Quarterly*, teaches one of the most notorious and sought after private fiction workshops in the country, and has written three story collections and five novels of his own, including *Dear Mr. Capote, Extravaganza, My Romance,* and most recently *Zimzum*, published last year by Pantheon. Lish's recent work is characterized by a frenzied and obsessional recursiveness, a syntax and diction that wheels along at the edge of sense and mystery, and an air of emotional desperation, of primal terror and self-horror at the verge of madness. Gordon, welcome to *The Book Show*.
Gordon Lish: Welcome to you, Douglas, in every sense. You failed to remark in your altogether too grand introduction of me that I am also your editor, or have been anyhow. I don't know if we'll ever have the occasion for this to occur again, but I think it's pertinent to remark so that the record is clear that I served as the editor for your remarkable novel *The Life and Times of Captain N.*

Glover: Thanks, Gordon. Which brings us to the sorry action of Knopf just a few weeks ago. Can you tell us what happened there?

Lish: It's difficult to say that it was "sorry." For in fact over the course of eighteen years I was free to operate in accordance with my instincts and my intuitions and to be rather remarkably free of any kind of governance respecting the profit and loss that my books would undergo. This would scarcely be news to anyone: they mainly underwent loss, I should expect. I would never really look closely enough at the receipts to have a precise reckoning of how matters fetched up in each instance. There may have been more instances of modest profits and of even break-even revenues, but certainly none of my books can be maintained to have helped to pay the light bill in the Random House building. No.

But I do think—and I want to remark this—that I am in a state of everlasting gratitude to my masters for having let me for so very long do what I did. And over the course of eighteen years, I think I was able to do not a little damage, and I am happy for that—damage in the sense that Nigel Kennedy means damage. I recall before coming to New York to take on the job at *Esquire,* where I was fiction editor for eight years, saying to my wife Barbara, who is recently deceased, that I hoped that I would one day have a station from which I could inflict rather a lot of damage on the national literature, and the post at *Esquire* as fiction editor, I think, gave me that opportunity. And then on a significantly wider scale Knopf did ditto. So that I really have no regrets. That all this was brought to an end did not occur to me as a great surprise. I thought my days were numbered.

Glover: I remember you remarking that before the event.

Lish: I've always had the sense that I exist in whatever post I occupy at the sufferance of my masters, so that I've really never felt that this was anything more than a temporary experience. But of course, that's what life is, is it not? One ultimately, if one's paying attention to reality, has his days on earth at the sufferance of masters infinitely greater than any that might be imposed on me at any office where I may come daily to do my labors. One answers always, ultimately, to Nature or, if one prefers, the notion of God. We're just visiting.

Glover: Correct me if I'm wrong, but you are not the only one let go in this?

Lish: So far as I know I was not the only one. I think there were quite a number of people who were dismissed; the bulk of them, I believe, worked in the Knopf juvenile division.

Glover: I see. But now you still have *The Quarterly*.
Lish: Yes. I publish *The Quarterly*, under the protection of the Rosencrantz Foundation, which picked up the magazine just subsequent to Vintage's having dropped it. Vintage being a division of Random House and currently under the imprimatur of the Knopf publishing group, so called, which consists of Knopf and Pantheon and Vintage. Vintage put out twenty-five numbers of *The Quarterly*, and then deemed that would be quite ample insofar as they were concerned. The magazine then fell under the protection of the Rosencrantz Foundation, where thus far two numbers have been published—Q26 and Q27—and very shortly Q28 will be brought out. This through the affiliation that *The Quarterly* has with The Gutter Press, which is largely a one-man operation sustained by a remarkably energetic fellow named Sam Hiyate up in Toronto.

Glover: What's happened at Knopf seems part and parcel with a number of attacks, bits of negative publicity, that have befallen you in the last couple of years. You've been attracting trouble or attracting cultural lightning. This reminds me of the position that Harold Bloom has in the culture at large. Somehow his public position, and your public position, attract not only public attacks but also personal attacks. Do you find that somewhat true?
Lish: It's curious you remarked this because Bloom and I had been great good pals for a good number of years, and that friendship came to a very abrupt end, not without relation to his publication of a list of writers to whom he proposed special attention be accorded. Given that the list included on it rather robustly non-bardic poets in the order of Rita Dove and failed to cite Jack Gilbert, for example, I found it a breach of judgement of an unforgivable kind. Such a breach was one of not a few of same, and I did not think that I could maintain relations with Bloom with honor. But I do think—I continue to think—that so much of what I feel applies to the matter of making sentences and of making one's way with sentences in the vicinity of difficult objects owes to my reading in Bloom, my reading in Denis Donoghue, my reading in Julia Kristeva. I think it's fair to say that these three writers have more potently shaped my feelings about what it is that my life has been given over to than any other writers I could point to. So my debt to Bloom is irredeemable, and I've always had the fondest feelings for him quite apart from his presence on the page. But I could not keep myself in a friendly relation with him subsequent to the list that he—for whatever reasons that he was persuaded to publish it—did publish.

But in respect of your specific remarks that Bloom and I seem in certain ways matched in the cynosure that we have seemed to express as targets for not a little criticism of a personal and public kind that tends to go over the top, I guess that may be the case, and that may in fact have something to do with what tended to cement our relations with one another. Now I tend to find myself on the side of those who would oppose him by reason of the remarks I just offered respective of the, I think, unlucky list. But it is fair to say—and I don't think this necessarily applies to Bloom—that the career I've had, for reasons I'm sure have mainly to do with my own rather neurotic conduct of my life, has not been easy. Long before I showed any kind of difficulties with the press in New York, or nationally, I had difficulties with other persons who had the power to offer up public opinions of my activities. This goes all the way back to my years teaching in California and before that. I think it's pertinent to remark that as long ago as 1961, or '62, I think it was, there was an article published in *The Nation* concerning my having been fired out of my post as a school teacher in California. *The Nation* in that instance took my part on the grounds that I wasn't opposing the California school system, conducting myself in a way that was congruent with *The Nation*'s principles. Then thirty years later, when I opposed *Harper's* magazine in a litigation concerning its abridgement of my copyright protections—at least so far as that was my argument in the courts, which argument was upheld by the courts—*The Nation* ran an editorial taking a view of that, which contradicted its old view and held that I was behaving improperly. But the sense I feel of being embattled, and the sense in which you construe Bloom's life as one which has been embattled, certainly is nothing new to me really, and I don't doubt for an instant that one has precisely the life that one wishes to have, and that I have been in everywise the creator of just these conditions. One has the sense that one has orchestrated the very conditions that close in around one, and, being the author of that, is the guilty party.

Glover: Do you think that this *agon*, this contest, that you have set up for yourself, fuels your own work? Your writing or teaching?
Lish: I don't think there's any question about that, Douglas. I think that quite plainly one is in a contest with one's father—I don't think I've ever really escaped that sense of my life, for as long as I can remember—one's father takes on various forms as one goes forward in life and however one may feel himself free, eventually, of his neuroticism, the delusion of that

freedom is brought home very forcefully day in and day out, if one pays any attention at all. That this dynamic should exist as the source of energy that somehow produces sentences for me in my own fictions is quite clearly the case. I think that all of my fictions tend to run a course pretty much of a kind. I don't think any of us really ever gets greatly distant from his rut; and that the grooves in which we have been operating for the very longest while should ever be somehow removed from us, or should melt away from beneath us, I think is quite a preposterous claim. One seeks to produce at least the effect of having gained some freedom, but it's never really the case in the end. You look back at the work and you can see how remarkably, remarkably, governed by the conditions it was. But, yes, what freedom I have had in the vicinity of my object, what small amount of deviation I have had from my destiny, I think I'm pleased to report has existed almost exclusively in my fictions. In class, I like to go to the blackboard and draw for my students a rather simple-minded diagram of a point rushing toward a gravitating object. Every effort that might be made in the course of their time with me to found some sort of deviation in their behavior, some sense of what their destiny would otherwise be, so that they in resisting it can produce some kind of freedom for themselves to perform on the page in a way that might give surprise, represents an angle of deviation no greater than ten or fifteen percent. But it is in the filling in of that space—if you could imagine a figure where you would have a scalene triangle covering the space between the fate that would otherwise be enjoyed and the fate that might be enjoyed by resisting one's fate—within that space, within that small triangle, there is enough freedom for all of us to do work that might contribute reasonably strongly to the national literature.

Glover: I should point out that on the dust jack of *Zimzum*, Don DeLillo says that you are famous for all the wrong reasons. I suppose he could have almost said "notorious" or "infamous," but implying that in fact the right reason would be your fiction, itself.

Lish: DeLillo has always been remarkably generous to me. He is my longest lasting and best friend—and I, with all shame, acknowledge that. Here is an instance when one's friend is publicly remarking on one's work to one's own benefit. But I think if anyone knows DeLillo, as I do, one knows that he's a man of such probity that friendship would not coerce him to behave in anywise other than how he would behave on the merits of the matter as he would judge them. But I think that's a great kindness for DeLillo to have said that. I take some pleasure in my work only in the abstract. When

I actually from time to time crack open a book of mine and look at a few sentences, I'm instantly overcome by the compilation of error that confronts me. I find it in the front, in fact. The work in theory—I like to think—has force and ought to exist, but when I go to it and look I'm appalled by all the wrongness that I see. But it's the best I've been able to do. I continue to try to do my best. I have, ever since the completion of *Zimzum*, been captured by a set of notions that I like to think of as a novel-in-progress. Although I've written probably two to three thousand pages of said novel or work-in-progress, nothing has really been adduced that I've been willing to live with. The notion of error simply multiplying, however greatly I might exert every energy to reduce its incidence, is I think ultimately prevailing over me. I seem not to be willing to live with the smallest error anymore, and that's proving almost uniformly interdictive of my efforts.

Glover: This is unusual in your writing process, to actually spin out that many pages.
Lish: Unusual, not at all. These terribly slim volumes that I have brought out really are the residue of what would otherwise be rather gargantuan volumes of work if I was more willing to live with what I produce. I am a great one for throwing away. I throw away and throw away and throw away. After I've thrown away and come to something that I think is plausible, I am a great one, then, for cutting like mad and have not infrequently—well into books in various permutations on the way to manufacture—cut extravagantly so that what may have begun as a three-hundred-page book became a two-hundred-page book and then a one-hundred-and-forty-page book and so on.

Glover: I know you do that also as an editor.
Lish: Yes, indeed.

Glover: And I remember when we were working on my book what you kept saying was to cut extraneous material in order to strive for a sense of mystery. Mystery seemed to have almost a technical meaning for you.
Lish: It does, it does.

Glover: Can you explain that before we close?
Lish: Yes of course. Let me get to the heart of the matter. I think it was Arthur Cohen who said most convincingly—and I only read this recently after some thirty years; I think I've been teaching for thirty-five years, and

maintaining this as a postulate in my teaching—Cohen said that the reader comes to a piece of writing not for sense but for time. He's looking for a way out of real time, he's looking to fall out of the complication of history, the complication of his life, and to enter a new time wherein the clock that will eventually tick off the last of his life is not keeping the measure, a species of timelessness in which we all of us are flowing free from the given conditions. We know this all too well from those moments of transcendence, those instants, those nanoseconds wherein we are lifted away from ourselves and from the agonies and experience of consciousness. I think that Cohen's argument is that art offers this opportunity for the transcendent experience, and is well-made when it keeps to its business of trying to produce precisely such an experience for those who come to it. To offer information, to offer sense, to offer meaning, is in fact, as a mathematical matter, to deprive the reader of this other experience, because the two can't really coexist. Of course, there is no way in which one can utter the language without reference, otherwise one has nonsense. So, to a great extent, whatever language one puts down is taxed by a certain amount of reference. The notion I back is that, to the extent one is able, one should suppress that information. By so doing, one heightens mystery.

A Conversation with Gordon Lish

Rob Trucks / 1996

From *The Pleasure of Influence: Conversations with American Male Fiction Writers* (Lafayette, IN: Purdue University Press, 2002), pp. 89–123. © 2002 Purdue University Press. Reprinted by permission.

This interview was conducted in 1996 and published in 2002.

"I believe that we all want to stick out in the world," Gordon Lish once said, "that the least of us has a profound impulse to distinguish himself from everyone else." "Sticking out" is the least of Gordon Lish's accomplishments. He is a near-mythic figure within New York literary circles as the most visible teacher and editor of American writing in the past thirty years.

Lish worked as an editor at *Esquire* and Knopf and was founding editor of *The Quarterly*. He taught at Yale and Columbia before taking his fiction workshops private, and several articles have referred to him as "the most sought after, most expensive" writing teacher in the nation.

As a fiction writer, Lish has published several books, most notably, *Dear Mr. Capote* and *Peru* as well as *Epigraph*, released just prior to this discussion. In the previous year Lish had signed an agreement with New York publishing house Four Walls Eight Windows to publish his new fiction, as well as revised editions of his earlier books.

This interview attempts to focus attention on Gordon Lish's writing rather than his other exploits. We met at the offices of *The Quarterly* on Manhattan's East Side in December of 1996 and, not surprisingly, talked for some time of writers and writing before the tape recorder was turned on.

Rob Trucks: You've done many interviews that have focused on your role as an editor and a teacher, and those roles can't be ignored in this conversation, but I would like to, as much as possible, focus this discussion on your writing.

Gordon Lish: Rob, I'm delighted that's the case. I'm all too often, I think, made to make responses in respect of my having edited and taught. In both of which instances I'm probably as despised as I am as a writer. I mean, it doesn't really matter. I'm not going to do any better in this category, but it's refreshing anyway. It's new.

Q: Your influence as an editor and a teacher has been well documented, but what writers have had an influence on your own work?
A: I think if I were to speak to the question of writers that have influenced me, it would be convenient to deflect the force of the question by citing philosophers I read who have, in fact, influenced me enormously, and I cite one of them, in fact, in the novel that brought you to my doorstep, *Epigraph*, which is to say Julia Kristeva with specific respect to her book *Powers of Horror*. But it's fiction writers that you're looking for.

Q: Not necessarily. Kristeva's obviously important and I'm certainly curious as to her influence. You mention her as far back as *Zimzum*, and she has the epigraph to *Epigraph*.
A: I want to make it very clear that her fiction has not amused me in any kind of way, but I'm able to read it. But, of course, I wouldn't even attempt to read it given that I would have to then be reading into English and I'm willing to take the view that any writing of any prospect of making its way with me would have to have been done in English. The kinds of things I'm looking for in a piece of writing can only have been put there by somebody writing in English, or writing in American English.

I read and reread Gilles Deleuze's *Thousand Plateaus*. I read everything I can by Deleuze and Guattari. Giorgio Agamben I've read all of and reread and am rereading now. That would be true of at least two Kristeva titles, *Powers of Horror* and *Strangers to Ourselves*. I think I've read that one three times. I've read all of Bloom several times. That is to say, I'm not interested in Bloom, the critic, but Bloom, the theoretician, yes. I've read all of Donoghue. I don't think there's anybody writing English sentences that produces better ones than Donoghue.

Q: The authors that you mentioned, except for Bloom and Donoghue, all write in other languages, yet you said that you were only interested in American fiction writers. That rule obviously doesn't apply to philosophy.
A: Yes, all are in translation with the sole exception of Bloom and Donoghue.

Among fiction writers, living fiction writers, none would be more immediately retrieved by me across that paddle of responses that would count more than DeLillo, surely. And then secondarily, Ozick. I would be a liar if I were to fail to remark the affection that I have had for certain of Harold Brodkey's short pieces, so called. As he himself was given defensively to observe, not all that short. I rather imagine that certain of Brodkey's short pieces probably surpass, in magnitude, my own novels, thinking of "Largely an Oral History of My Mother," of the story "S. L."

These pieces, incidentally, appeared, and one wants to underscore this observation, for malicious reasons, in *The New Yorker*, under the editorship of Bill Shawn. One wonders if *The New Yorker*, by implication I suppose my observations suggest, would publish such work now. I know they were happy and delighted to publish Brodkey's pieces on his dying of AIDS, which I didn't think quite fit the bill for me.

But in any case, I read Brodkey's novel, *A Party of Animals*, in manuscript, over the course of one night, starting as soon as I got home from my office, having been given the manuscript by Bob Gottlieb, not by Brodkey, whose editor I was officially at the time, and the gist of that is that Brodkey's delivering his manuscript to Gottlieb was his way of severing relations with me, although later on he elected to repair that severance. Not all that effectively certainly, and not in a way that would interest us here. But the point is that I took the manuscript home that night, started reading it about seven and, despite the distractions of family life, stayed with it, I suppose, pretty incessantly until ten in the morning, having completed the reading of well over a thousand pages and coming to the view that this was the surpassing novel by an American of the century.

I would now amend that view, holding Cormac McCarthy's *Blood Meridian* for that post, for that distinction, if my reading of these things has any value at all.

You're speaking to me on a day when I feel myself rather more vacant from myself than I have ordinarily felt, but each day I'm getting the sense of my losing my purchase on that personality that I had sought so hard to disguise myself within and to present myself under the auspices of, and I don't do that anymore, or I'm losing my grasp on that presentation of myself, and I'm willing to therefore offer, with my comments, the ironic interpretation that they may be completely without value. I mean, everybody else may come to that view, but I know I have come more and more, certainly, to that view.

But anyhow, "influence" is a considerable word and requires every kind of examination, and one does not want to give it, but in an "in my face" or "in your face" kind of way, Brodkey's fictions and DeLillo's fictions and Ozick's fictions and McCarthy, with particular respect to that book *Blood Meridian* and alternatively *Outer Dark*, I find them unbudgeable acmes of expression in the language and cannot claim, as distant as my work may seem from any of the aforementioned, that they are not, to a greater extent than anything else I might posit, on my mind as I write. Is this work, in its appetite, rather to say its absence of appetite, does it make a legitimate claim to a place in the national literature alongside a *Blood Meridian*? That's a most disturbing question.

What I'm trying to get at is that what I want from my own activities as a writer is, to put it plainest, everything. What I want is some kind of sufficiency in reply to the incommensurable insult of death. I want everything from the page and reckon that, even though my everything may be an entirely different coloration than McCarthy's everything, there is an absolutism, or ultimacy, in which these artifacts can be measured, one to the other. To find oneself insufficient in the face of that, insufficient in the face of DeLillo's 1,414-page manuscript for the novel *Underworld* or DeLillo's *Mao II*, which I've just read for the fourth time, it is distracting at the very least.

Is it disabling? Not quite disabling. So it appears because I continue to scribble away, and not without, I beg you to believe, the intention that the mark made by those works will be competitive. I don't wish to make the claim that my aims exist apart from what is also in that category. I'm not willing to say that I write for myself. I'm not willing to say I write for God. I'm not willing to say I write without a great concern to see the work translated into time and space and therefore occupying, maybe not making, a place for itself with other works that have made themselves.

I don't think I will ever, given on the one hand the terms of my ambitions and on the other hand the terms of my limitations, however much I may believe absolutely in the Swinburnian notion that one stands on his limitation, one stands on his limitude, and in standing on his limitude, one shall be as lavish as one requires. It's only from standing on one's limitude that one can achieve that absolute lavishness. Despite all that, I'm not disabled but am much dismayed to reckon with my failing limitations, my failing powers to face my limitations, as measured against the acmes that I've remarked: DeLillo, Brodkey, McCarthy, and Ozick.

Q: What is your greatest limitation as a writer?
A: I'm a small man. I believe that the body is continuous with the sentence at its best. I don't have the stamina, the physical strength to produce the kind of text that persons in better possession of their bodies would have.

You know, my friend DeLillo can get out and run six miles. He's not as big a man as Brodkey is or as Cormac McCarthy is. I've seen McCarthy and he's a fairly sizable fellow. There's something to it, in my judgment. How does this speak to the matter of gender I immediately am made to wonder, but we're not going to engage that topic, I do hope. But I can make the claim for myself that my body precedes me out of the page, and with all the vicissitudes that have always interfered with its translation into what's exterior, my having had disfiguring skin disease all my life, my having been a little guy, and therefore extremely, extremely dexterous in beating big guys in games until I got to a certain age when bigness mattered more than skill mattered, more than adroitness mattered, or deftness mattered.

What I think is my defect now, as I'm able to examine my experience as a writer now, is that I've passed that point where mere adroitness, mere deftness will do, and massiveness, size, bulk, and all of the vulgarity of that notion is certainly the ground on which I hold myself to failure. And the work will always fail on account of that.

Q: Then wouldn't logic argue that your earlier writings, when you were likely in better physical shape, come closer to the vibrancy, the absolute you're trying to achieve?
A: It doesn't. I've looked at it. I've had the luck, under the agreement made with Four Walls, to look at the early work and revise the hell out of it, and I know I'm infinitely more able now than I was then, but that ability is all craft. It's not desire.

Q: The ability is deftness?
A: That's what it is. It's just adroitness. I know the moves now. I know how to make it down the court and elude those who would interfere with me, but whether I can make the kind of score that I wanted to make, that I set out to make, producing on the page the vision that brought about the impulse, that's another question entirely.

My physical response to *Blood Meridian* is, "Gee, that's my kind of stuff." That's wall to wall my kind of stuff, and I would be competent of being driven by a notion like that but absolutely incompetent of bringing it to bear, bringing it into any kind of compositional reality. I couldn't do it. And if I produced five hundred pages of that, I'd probably end up reducing it to fifty pages.

Q: But the fact is that *Blood Meridian* is beyond the capabilities of ninety-nine percent of us. Is it a sin that neither you nor I will produce a *Blood Meridian*?
A: It is, Rob. It is. For me, it is. If we take the view that the only reason to do this is to somehow make a reply, make a reasonable reply to the unreasonable character of existence, to time, because that's what animates me, then we're in the realm of ultimate matters. We're in the realm of absolute matters, and it's precisely that McCarthy does what ninety-nine percent cannot do that makes it the only thing to be done. It's necessity itself to somehow seek to surpass McCarthy.

Q: Doesn't that take us too far into the realm of competition?
A: It's all about competition. I'm all about competition. The horror of that is, since I invoke that, it's precisely that view that undoes me. If I could take a more libertarian view about myself, if I could be more forgiving, if I could say, "Well, there's a kind of thing that I do and it's forgivable if I do that kind of thing as well as I am able," I'm left entirely dissatisfied with the experience. It isn't enough for me. I'm the kind of person who if I come to the shopping mall, when the sign says, "Something for Everybody," I immediately want to rewrite that, to revise the statement to read, "Everything for Gordon." And that's the kind of shopping mall I want to be in.

Q: But aren't we doomed for failure if we realized at the outset that we cannot achieve *Blood Meridian*?
A: But somebody did. But somebody did, you see. Somebody did. A man did it. Somebody wrote *Moby Dick,* one has to remind oneself.

Q: But isn't there pleasure in achieving as absolute a work of fiction as you yourself are capable of?
A: Only defeat. Only defeat because it is, again, the affirmation of nature, of time that you are not enough. You are not sufficient. You are defective through and through. You die. No, it is not acceptable to me that I be served up my portion since the receipts that I will eventually be given by time exceed my portion. All shall be taken from me, and I need all right now.

I want all the women. I can recall when I was twelve, thirteen years old having the view that the only prospect that was reasonable would be that I would bed all the women. I don't know what this meant to me at age twelve and thirteen. I know that there was a joke that was commonly about in those days about a guy that was whacked out who had precisely the same vision. But I've been locked up twice and probably not for trying to bed all the women but for having notions that it was a doable thing.

I continue at age almost sixty-three to feel that it's a kind of no-option situation since my construction of life is a sort of no-option situation. Nevertheless, given the alibi of psychopathology, I'm not daunted by this. I mean, I'm not daunted by the absolute numbers, by your making the claim that, "Well, Gordon, *Blood Meridian* was done by the rarest fellow under the rarest circumstances in the rarest moment." He may not be competent of that accomplishment now. He probably could not do it again. But I have yet to exceed myself, to cross a line as uncrossable as that.

I think that's the only thing. I'm not satisfied with anything less. If I were a larger man, then maybe. This is where we return to the weird politics of the body. I've made the claim that the accomplishment of the unaccomplishable act may be a function of the body, a sufficient body, and I feel I have an insufficient body. If I were a larger man, I might be willing to forego that absolutism in respect of accomplishment. I might be willing to be satisfied with less than myself on the page, feeling I had more of myself in reality. But I feel myself actually excavated. I feel myself, placed by reason of circumstance, on the margins in both realms, and I have in me all the frustration, all the rage, all the anger, all the viciousness of temperament that is the result of that sense of myself having been thrust to the margins, by reason, not of ability, but of the given.

Q: You mentioned your presentation of yourself. In your fiction you consistently mix the obviously autobiographical with the not-so-obviously autobiographical. Is this an attempt to re-create or remake yourself?
A: Everything I do is an effort to remake myself. I'm not interested in remaking anybody else, and I'm not interested in re-creating anything outside of myself. I'm interested in finding, on the page, a replacement for what I feel I've been deprived of in actuality. But I beg you to believe that when you say "obvious autobiographical elements," I would refuse that observation and say "apparent autobiographical elements."

Q: Well, I'm referring to more than using your own name as the name of your protagonist. I'm talking about things such as using your own neighborhood as the setting or the names of your own father and mother as the names of the protagonist's father and mother.

A: I have two ways of answering this, or three ways. Let me give you three notions that I think probably apply to what I'm up to. One is, if I can set forth certain facticities that are somewhat known of me, then I can buttress the force of authority in those absolute inventions that I'm going to set forth. So that's one trick. In the case of *Peru*, for example, I dedicated the book to my mother and father, gave their actual names so I could use the actual names in the book to give some sense of authority to the claim that I had, at the age of six, or the speaker had, at the age of six, done away with another boy. I gave the name of the person who was presumably assassinated in the course of the book, Stephen Michael Adinoff, and his dates, trying to lend a certain verifiable force to the fictions that have been assembled around the facticities.

I do it, too, because I think it's pointless to invent certain points. The energy that is consumed in the invention, I think, is quite uselessly consumed. Why bother to invent? The whole thing is a fiction by my lights. Everybody knows it's made up. Why play the game? If it's a novel, if it's being promoted as a novel, it's being put out there or sponsored as a novel, then presumably it's all made up, is it not, so why bother?

Q: While you're at this point, "being promoted as a novel," in what way is *My Romance* a novel?

A: In what way is it a novel? Only because I said it's a novel. I think the book says it's a novel. It may not be a novel. I don't know how I would define what a novel is. I know people spend a lot of time with that activity. I don't know if it's interesting anymore.

I read recently a book I'm rather fond of, Seamus Deane's *Reading in the Dark*. I'm told that it was originally published as a memoir in England or in Ireland and is being published as a novel here. Does it interfere with my savor of the text to know that in one instance it's to be viewed in this category? I must say, "Yes. Yes, it does." Had I known it was viewed as a memoir and then later published as a novel for reasons that may or may not have to do with literary gamesmanship, I might not have been so disturbed by the discovery.

These books that I put out are only novels by declaration. Are they novels by definition? Are they novels by construction? Heavens, I would be the last one to be competent to say. Certainly any of the critics that I've named that take their chicken and peas in the United States would say no. I mean, I imagine that Harold Bloom and Denis Donoghue would say that's just Gordon doing what Gordon does, but it's scarcely to be viewed as a novelistic enterprise. But I think I might persuade Julia Kristeva of a different view, or I might be able to persuade Giorgio Agamben, certainly, of a different view.

I don't think anything on that score is particularly new, by the way. I mean, this has been done for a long, long, long, long time. I'm not a scholar with sufficient information to give you names and addresses, but what I'm up to, or what I appear to be up to, the seeming actuality of so much that I put on the page, as in *My Romance,* has been done for a longish, longish, longish time while under the rubric of novel or imaginative writing.

My Romance turns on my turning my father upside down while he was perceived to be coughing, undergoing a coughing fit, and dropping him while doing that, and having had the inspiration to turn him upside down by reason of his having told the story over and over again of having done so to a brother who was choking on a peanut or a sourball or a piece of jelly apple or something in the park. The observation I might make about that, and this is interesting to me, is that it represents that particular mechanism, that device, precisely the mechanism that I apply in *Epigraph*—and I see it everywhere in me, the inability to escape my own devices.

Clearly, what study of any of these works sufficiently would discover, as I am now discovering since I'm revising them all, is that I'm quite unequipped to escape certain rather well-worked grooves in my personality when I perceive myself as the one speaking. These are the things I say, and I say them again and again and again and again, hoping each time to say them somewhat more ably than I have said them. But the fact that I am saying them over and over again certainly speaks to an authenticity in them. It certainly must speak to some kind of deeply positioned autobiographical stance. So I can't deny it, can I? I can't deny it. So there we are. Even in the effort to reinvent and write another autobiographical novel, as *Epigraph* might be construed to be, I'm back in the same place again.

I've only got two or three, not even themes. I've only got two or three, not even tales to tell. There are two or three bits that I can't let go of because they won't let go of me. But let me put this to you. The force of their fascination for me is certainly vouchsafed by my inability to escape them. I do try. I do try to elude the purchase taken on me by that which has developed in me, the jeopardy of the gaze. I do try to do that, but I don't succeed. Does anyone succeed at this? I'm not a close enough student of anyone's writing, or I'm too polite, despite what's claimed of me, to offer an observation yea or nay. I'm not willing to believe I'm unique in this respect.

I might have been able to get away with it better had I been a poet. I read Wallace Stevens a lot, since you asked about influence. I read Stevens's letters a lot. I'm eager to find all sorts of connections between Stevens's life and my own, right down to, and I'll put this to you, my extraordinary discovery not long ago that the face on the coin, on the half dollar coin, and on the dime that I gazed at so often as a child in honor of my idea of an American woman, since I come from an immigrant family, what a great American woman looked like, the one that you would have to bed in lieu of all other women you could not bed, turns out to have been modeled for a sculptor who was a landlord in Chelsea. He was, in fact, Stevens's landlord when he and Elsie Kachel, his wife, were living in Chelsea, and the design on the coin was modeled by Stevens's wife, so that it's fair to make the claim that I was infatuated with Stevens's wife, or at least her profile, from the time I was five or six or seven years old. You looked at the dime, you looked at the half dollar, and you saw Stevens's wife, amazingly.

When I say influence in this respect, what got me on this stream of discourse was what I would take to be repetitive fascinations, or fascinations surfacing again and again and again and again, in Stevens. I think we're rather more willing to forgive the poet than we are to forgive the novelist. But I'm probably not a novelist, and I'm probably not a poet either.

Talking to you now, the responses I make to you, as much as they seem to rush out of me without very careful consideration, are very practiced. I'm not surprising myself. I'm not saying anything that I haven't really probably said, one way or another, before. What I produce for the page probably comes a little closer, a little closer, to getting rid of, or squandering, something actual in myself and the pleasure I take from this, the way in which it answers the aggressivity in me, to use Kristeva's term from the first epigraph, is as close as I'm going to get to the sublime. I feel good with it. I've come to the view, with the work that I do, that it has finally become absolutely necessary for me to do it and that if I am made to see, five years after the work has achieved print, that I've simply iterated, yet again, an earlier reiteration, I'm not dismayed by it.

It seems to me that if the task is to write my name onto the surface of the earth, which I take to be as hard a surface as we will find, then the effort of scribing the same mark over and over and over again might leave some kind of trace. And I think that's what I'm doing, writing the same mark over and over and over again.

Q: When you say writing the same mark over and over again, are you making the same effort, are you using the same muscles when you begin a novel that you use when you're rewriting, for example *Dear Mr. Capote,* which you've recently done?

A: Best question I was asked Rob. Best question anybody ever asked me. I use my dick, mainly, to write the first time, and I'm using my brains to do the revisions. I mean, not my brain. I'm using rather practiced sequences of motions that have to do chiefly with mind or chiefly with know-how. I'm trying to stick it into the page the first time out. The twenty-eight versions of *Epigraph*, each of which was disposed of and each of which, I would argue, is a distance from its predecessor—I disposed of them entirely because I'm trying to create a blank, but I couldn't create that blank, quite plainly. Never could create that blank. They were done with an effort to jam it in as deeply as I could.

There in fact is, it occurs to me now, quite felicitously, a little moment in the book when the speaker, which I find to be the delicate way to mark the narrator, is discussing the pressure that is produced between the unmentionables, I think is his word, his own unmentionable and his sex partner's unmentionable, by reason of her gesture with her heels. She's able to enact some kind of gesture with her heels and his ankles such that the contact between them is tighter. I'm always looking for that tighter and tighter and tighter contact. I find that in actual sex, it's never quite considerable enough. And I'm not talking about a psychic or spiritual or an emotional experience. I'm talking about simply the body being in contact with its other never being quite sufficient to satisfy me. I never feel like I'm in enough, man. I'm always afraid that she's going to say, "Are you in yet?"

Q: Does the analogy hold true with your work? Are you ever afraid that the book is going to voice back, Are you in yet?
A: Oh, man. Do you know what? This is it. Given the terms that I've invoked by reason of everything I've said, I think you've offered the supreme reply to my work.

I would like to not only put the steak and potatoes out there but to gobble them all up, gobble up everything on the table, and everybody else's food, too, put my hands on their plate and eat their food, as well. So yes, the book's saying, "Yes Gordon, tell me when you're in." That's probably it. I'm just going to have to deal with that. I don't know what else to do.

But do you know who's in? Certainly McCarthy. Certainly in *Blood Meridian*. I would say he's really in in *Blood Meridian*, and DeLillo's really in in *Underworld*.

Q: I want to talk about the revision process and editing your own work but, while we're talking about *Epigraph* specifically, you said that there are twenty-eight. Would we call them drafts or versions?

A: I wouldn't call them drafts. I never sit down with ambition to produce something that I'll then rid myself of or keep some semblance of and work through and improve. No, I write it as ably as I can, as truly as I can, as carefully, as closely machining a sentence with a ferocity of attention that I would hold to be as good as you're going to get, as good as I'm going to get, ever.

Q: So there were twenty-eight previous versions of *Epigraph* before the one that was published?
A: What you're holding in your hand is twenty-nine. It's a completely different undertaking. From start to finish a different rendering. This is the only one that turned out to be epistolary.

Q: Really?
A: It never was epistolary until I did the last one and then that I revised and revised. The process I undergo usually is when I get it back in type the first time round, I do about eighty percent of it all over again.

Q: Is *Epigraph* your greatest accomplishment as a writer? Is it the closest you've come to that absolute as a writer?
A: Oh God, I hope not, man.

Q: If you had to hand over one of your books as an example of your finest effort toward the absolute, which one would you choose?
A: I won't dodge the question because I'm always of the view that I'm about to crap out and whatever I've gotten on the record is it. It would be improper to point to something yet unwritten, and the work presently underway, *Arcade*, even though I'm up to rather a lot of pages is, God knows, not for the record yet. But there's a book called *Self-Imitation of Myself*.

I can't recite the title without offering the observation that DeLillo abominates that title, and maybe that's the reason why I insist upon it now, so as to avoid any taint of being influenced by DeLillo although he's influenced me a lot in respect to very specific matters. I asked him recently about an epigraph for the novel *Arcade*. It's a completely contrived epigraph, by the way, but assigned to somebody. I do that from time to time. I'm a bad guy, Rob. But that's all right. I mean, it's a novel, right?

It's a book that, in fact, Four Walls has their hands on. I finished it about a year ago, I think it is. I finished a novel called *Chinese* and a novel called *Self-Imitation of Myself,* and I haven't read either one of them. I don't really want to read *Chinese* at all. I imagine I'll be much displeased when I do read it, but I have a sense that *Self-Imitation of Myself* would probably be that book that I would put before you as that object, making the claim that it not so much expresses my best token in the game, but it probably encompasses the heart of me better than anything I've ever done.

Q: Will the words "a novel" be printed beneath the title?
A: Yes, otherwise I'd probably be put away in jail forever. Now I haven't looked at it, mind you, since that occasion of desire when I believed I was in as far as I could've got in and she was screaming with completion and perfection of all her wants. When we have a look at the matter, she may make claim "Were you there? Did anything happen? Tell me when it's over."

Q: So *Self-Imitation* is still a dick book?
A: It's a dick book. All my books are dick books.

Q: But much time has passed since the original appearance of *Dear Mr. Capote* and you've gone back and revised it. Doesn't that make the reprint a brain book?
A: It sure does and they all will become, but you know they're infinitely better reflections of my concerns for cadence, my concerns for the syntactical relations that might be achieved. They've been spot-cleaned of their errors to the extent I'm able, but the initial error, the original error, where I wanted to put my dick in the first place, there's the thing. Where you want to put your pencil in the first place occurs to me as critical, and it's probably there that I'm never going to escape.

Here, I'll tell you something I haven't told anyone. My original fascination, the thing that set me in motion, the thing I wanted to write about with this book, *Epigraph*, was produced in a glance. I think it's referred to in the most passing way in the novel that now obtains, or the work that now obtains if you'll grant me that, but at a certain point, at the initial point, when the originary moment was upon me, this was it. My wife was being held aloft by two nurses and a third person. It may have been a mother. I don't know who the third person was in the room with her, but there were two nurses and a third person. She was strangling on her saliva. All the material in her bowels was running out of her anus. She was urinating. Everything was coming out of everywhere. Suction tubes were in her everywhere. She had tubes in her chest, two tubes in her chest, and because she could no longer flex her feet, given the nature of the disease which had made the muscles in her feet useless, they had fixed in a certain position. She was positioned on her toes. The most excruciating pain one would imagine. She could no longer speak, of course. She could not even scream her agony. And I was rushing back and forth from the closet in the kitchen to the bathroom adjoining our bedroom, where my wife was, with towels. We always had stacks to clean up and clean up and clean up. And she must have, at the time, weighed forty, forty-five, fifty pounds.

I've never seen anything like it, never imagined, and I've been in two bughouses, been in jail. I'm willing to look at anything. I've looked at hard things in my life, but I never imagined I would see anything quite so close to a transfiguring moment as this. This was as close as I have ever come to seeing the unseeable. I looked at this thing and felt such shame in looking at it. I had the sense of such deep-seated shame in looking upon her nakedness in this way. This was a nakedness of the spirit. I don't even have that termed. I would have to try to write it out and write it out and write it out.

But that's what animated me in the moment. I thought, "That's the thing." That was the aspect. Not my wife, not the three people, but just what I was able to sense, the "on the toesness." Her "on the toesness." "On the toesness" is the only way to say it. It was her "on the toesness." It was the bones. It was the death head, the mouth open and everything rushing out all over the body. I wanted to make a book out of that. I wanted to make a book out of that and my looking at it. I wanted to make a book out of my sense of being unable to achieve contact between my unmentionable and that unmentionable. I wanted to make a book about my being kept out of it, at a distance from it, and because of being kept out of it, at a distance from it, everlastingly ashamed, everlastingly damned in my judgment. Damned.

I couldn't do that. I tried. I don't know how many of those twenty-eight books we've been talking about were efforts to do that, but I certainly couldn't get anywhere close to it. I beg you to believe all of them were efforts to reduce the whole of the event to a wispiness of it that I'm not even competent to describe to you. All of it achieved in the glance, and certainly vividly. I mean, I'm still able to look exactly at the thing I was looking at then, and able to revisit the same feelings I had then. It's not as if I've lost it, but what has occurred is a failure before it, an insufficiency before the force of the object, and it's important that I make the point, the object is not something which would be describable by anybody else but myself, and only to be seen in capturing that fraction of a second when that certain composition of elements was as it were and as I was in relation to them. That's what I mean by the object.

Q: Is the incapability of rendering that moment, that vision, that feeling of shame—is that a temporary incapability? Is that something that you couldn't achieve with this book? Is that something you will ever be able to capture?
A: Rob, I don't know. I will try. I will try. I'll never have another one like that and I can't do that one again. I failed that one. I contaminated it. I can speak to it as I'm doing with you now. I may find myself speaking to it, but I'll never render it.

Now, I beg you to believe that part of that sense of failure certainly derives out of my knowing, absolutely knowing, that DeLillo, that Brodkey, that McCarthy would not fail in the face of those objects. They could do it. I certainly would include Ozick in that, but I'm not prepared to go beyond that and say that Denis Johnson, for example, who we both admire very greatly, could do it or any other persons we've been naming could do it.

I think maybe Barry Hannah could do it because Barry Hannah has an enormous heart and he's afraid of nothing. I recall Donoghue once saying about Barry Hannah, when I think I was publishing Hannah's *Airships*, Barry Hannah is afraid of nothing in experience. I try to be afraid of nothing in experience, but I'm really afraid of everything. I try to adopt this disguise I'm afraid of nothing. I like to say I've been in the bughouse twice. I've been in jail. I've done some heavy stuff. I've driven across country a number of times with Cassady, that kind of shit, but the fact of the matter is I'm afraid of everything. Everything. Principally, I'm of afraid of her saying, "Tell me when you're in," you know. That kind of thing.

I'm terribly afraid of anything exterior of myself and have always been. I've never not been afraid. I've always been uncomfortable. I've never not been uncomfortable. I've always been uncomfortable with my body. I've always been uncomfortable with the earth, and I can't seem to ever find my way on the page outside of the pressure of those repressed powers, of those repressed forces in me. That's what I'm all about. I'm all about my fear. I would like to make the claim that the desire in me is adequate to displace the fear in order to produce a text but always, at the end of the text, when I come back to it, and I'm coming back to *Capote* now, I see that fear really won out.

Q: Fear affects your writing, but does or did fear ever affect you when you acted as editor?
A: No. I'm tyrannical. I'm certainly reported to be tyrannical and everybody can't be wrong.

Q: I'm assuming that no one else edits your work.

A: You know, I was edited once. No one edits my work in the sense that I have edited others, line-by-line editing, no. But I'll tell you one time I was edited and I knuckled under, and it kills me that I did it and it's lost now forever. I can recall being told by somebody when I told the story that I should answer now with revision, but I couldn't do it when I got *Capote.* But it had to do with *Capote* and it had to do with the editor then, Billy Abrams, calling me at the last minute because I had gone through many, many revisions, and then saying, You know, I don't want this last one. I want the one before the last one.

I said, "No, no." The last one is the one that's the way I want it, and I just can't have it any other way, and what the last one was was a kind of frame over frame over frame, the unfolding of the guy who was claiming to be killing people. He suddenly shuts up in mid-sentence, and a letter to Mailer occurs and it's myself writing to Mailer about a bet we had about memory, trying to recall some responses to some trivia questions about soap operas and the claim being made to see if the narrative structure will produce recollections of a kind. It had to do maybe with what Ben Bernie would say or what Ben Bernie's sign-off was, I can't recall, but you get a letter to Mailer, a quite civilized letter to Mailer, about that discussion we had, and we had the bet, and I win the bet because here, in fact, is the proper answer to the question. And then it comes back to the novel as the novel is going forward again, and then it comes back to Mailer again—it was very, very carefully worked out. Minor, minor citations in a novel that was going along became major citations in the letter and vice versa, so that what was foregrounded was backgrounded, what was backgrounded was foregrounded. It was kind of a playful thing like that.

But Abrams said, "No, no. Nobody can read that. Nobody will ever get that and I don't know why you want to do that, and I don't want that, and it can't be that way." And I said, "I'm sorry, it can't be any other way but that way." And Lynn Nesbitt, who was my agent at the time, in essence she and her colleague suggested to me that I was being a fool, but I think I was a fool for allowing them to suggest that to me and for taking their counsel but did as told and Abrams had his way with it, and I always have been displeased.

When I've told the story, I think I've told it once or twice, I told it to one of my children once, and that child said, "Gee Dad, now that you've got a chance to do it your own way, do it your own way," and I couldn't. I couldn't. I thought about doing it when I redid *Capote* and I couldn't. My heart wasn't in it anymore. I just couldn't. No, that's an unsatisfactory way of making the statement. The fact of the matter is I couldn't do it. Mechanically I couldn't do it. Whatever intricacy then obtained in the making of that device required of me a kind of faith I no longer had.

Q: I want to talk about the dualities you mentioned in relation to fear restricting you as a writer. Can you not get Gordon Lish the writer out of the room and leave the manuscript with Gordon Lish the editor? Is it impossible for you to achieve that objectivity?
A: I can't do for myself what I have done for others. And I say with some satisfaction I've done some remarkable things for others.

Q: And you don't trust anyone else to do it for you?
A: I would be willing, perhaps, to do so if someone would volunteer, but nobody really ever has.

Q: Have you asked or are you expecting a knock on the door?
A: Well, I always knocked on doors. I knocked the house down. I was unwilling to get out of the picture. I had to have it right, my idea of right. Otherwise I couldn't put my name on that contract as it were. And I no longer have that kind of ferocity.

Q: In your short story, "How to Write a Novel" from *What I Know So Far*, you say to buy the first one of whatever it is because the maker of it is never going to knock himself out like that again. And yet you're rewriting your previously published books. So, should I believe you now, or should I believe you then?
A: Don't believe me anytime, Rob. Don't believe me anytime. Don't believe me anytime. I don't think I'm worth believing. There's no profit in believing me. The only thing you can get from it or not get from it is the pleasure of the time, the savor of the time. Because I'm a frightened man, because I'm essentially a weasel, because I'm essentially a swindler, because I'm a wheedler, because I'm always looking for a way to escape, I'm not reliable. I'm not trustworthy. I would make that claim of myself with anything I say, but in my life, in my relations, I've proved remarkably reliable. A good old loyal dog. I would never leave a wife. I've been left by wives. I would never leave a friend. I've been left by friends. So, reliable in human relations curiously but not reliable in what I say.

Language, for me, is something that belongs to other people. In the same way I feel that my body represents a bad judgment made on me. I should've looked like Alan Ladd. That was the notion I had as a kid. I should've looked like Alan Ladd. That would've been fair, that would've been just it seems to me. I should've been able to hit a baseball, I should've been able to knock them down the way Joe Louis could knock them down, that's the sense of sufficiency I have. I'm an American boy like that, and I think we're all American boys like that. My complaint is that when it comes to language, because of the kind of circumstances I came from, where English was not really a language that was exquisitely managed in the household, everything in me, always, everything in me is an effort to grab onto what I feel I was deprived of.

I can reduce it to the personification of Miss McEvoy, who is really Miss Donnelly in *Peru*. There really was a teacher I had named Miss McEvoy who was everything I understood Americans to be. She looked like Wallace Stevens's wife on the fifty-cent piece, and she sounded like Miss McEvoy, and she had the elocution of Miss McEvoy, and she had the enunciation of Miss McEvoy, and she had the syntax of Miss McEvoy and all of that. And because I feel myself, when I'm with the language, concerned only with how the language manifests itself through the conduit of Gordon Lish, I'm indifferent entirely to what's said. I don't even know what I'm saying half the time. I'm only saying it for the sake of saying it, for the sake of saying something, hoping that I can keep talking until I can get out of there safely, without somebody capturing me, without somebody seizing me by the throat.

You know, there's a story by Philip Roth that deserves reading. It's called "On the Air." He never quite finished it, I don't believe. And that tale concerns the terror of the Jew who's captured by the non-Jew, and all of whose Jewishness is really the consideration at hand. We got you now. You can't escape. We're going to measure your balls now.

At a certain point he crosses the George Washington Bridge. He thinks he has an engagement with Einstein at Princeton. Einstein's become the Jewish answer man. He feels there's an insufficiency of Jews on radio. Einstein's the smartest guy in the world. The Jews will have an answer man. So he's on his way to meet with Einstein to produce this program and never makes it. On the way, he's captured and dragged into a back room somewhere, and he's made to have his testicles weighed to see if they measure up.

Now I'm telling you, this is choice. It must be, in every Jew's terror, that this will be his destiny, that this will be fate. Somehow the most intimate part of himself will be measured against other men and found wanting. See? That's the thing. And whether it has any kind of reality to it, whether it has anything other than just simply phantasm to it, is not the point. The phantasm is good enough for me. I've been that way all my life. All my life. And language would be the domain in which I could fear myself most likely to be exposed.

I have seen myself on television and I'll make some error. I'll say something either factually wrong or rhetorically wrong or grammatically wrong and even be corrected, or I'll stop myself and make the correction or the interviewer corrects me. I'm always at the precipice of being convicted.

Q: How do you rationalize the difference between your feelings of responsibility for the spoken word and the written word? What's the difference between your feeling for the spoken word and your feeling for the written word?
A: Well, I'm better defended in the latter case. I'm much better defended and therefore the aggression in me, because, really, my fear must be, certainly, a version of my aggression. I'll answer your question in a moment. There's an observation I have that interests me a lot, and I've only made it recently about myself.

I walk along the sidewalk always, certainly in New York where the sidewalks are canted so that the rain runs off into the street. I try always to hold to the higher ground so I will, as I pass people, appear to myself to be taller than I am, so I will always seek to walk inside toward the storefronts. When I was in San Francisco recently, I felt how awful it was to be deprived of that advantage because the sidewalks weren't canted in the same way, so that you were often, likely, on the same footing as everybody else and I didn't like that. I wanted a little advantage to what I felt was my insufficiency.

And while I was thinking about that, as I was making my way, I was uncertain about where I was going. I would stop and ask people and, the most curious thing, I'm invariably smaller than the persons I'm asking, irrespective of gender, and I imagine myself as a mild and gentle and pacific man but invariably, and this has been true all of my life, I felt on the occasion of coming up to somebody to ask the question, that I'm somehow dangerous. That they perceive me as dangerous and that I have to, in asking the question, somehow give them to understand they are not to interpret my behavior as dangerous. And when I had this notion of myself, when I suddenly realized something about myself, because I'm not, despite evidence to the contrary, evidence you may take to the contrary, I'm not an introspective person at all. I don't sit around thinking about myself. I'm not competent. I would rather hide from myself than think about myself, so this came to me as really news. Wow! Why do I always think I'm dangerous when I'm a little guy? And I do think of myself as somehow dangerous to others. I don't doubt that it's because of the enormous aggression within me or aggressivity within me.

Q: But you're not bothered by that perception at all. Aren't you in a sense flattered that others would see you as dangerous?
A: Yes. I'm not so sure other people see me as dangerous. I see myself as being dangerous and trying to, in the moment of contact, disabuse them of the notion that I'm dangerous but really, probably, as you quite rightly surmised, relishing that this is an issue, relishing the prospect of this being an issue. And I probably have presented myself that way my whole life long. It's probably what got me into the jams I've gotten into in my life, gotten me the reputation I've got. Probably certainly what's gotten me able to be pals with certain persons you wouldn't think a New York Jewboy would end up being pals with. Probably because I've projected an air of a certain danger or recklessness or willingness to cross certain lines.

Now, I must beg you to believe, nothing in others is more terrifying to me. But I used to ride with guys like this. I was a wrangler in Tucson. I used to ride with whacked guys who didn't use saddles and didn't use regular tack and hit the horses with sticks and didn't come from Wyoming. They came from Long Island and couldn't wait to hurt somebody. I seem to have, in me, by reason of my sense of being tiny, of being small, of being insufficiently large for the case, an awful lot of violence and hence my absolute devotion to *Blood Meridian* as the supreme American text.

Q: Let's go back. You seem to be able to let the spoken word fall where it may yet you're extremely careful with the printed word.
A: I'm careful with the spoken word, too. I'm just very good at this. You've got to understand, man, you're talking to somebody who gets up once a week and talks for eight hours nonstop and sometimes does it three or four days in a row, so either I'm very good at it or I think I'm very good at it.

Q: You don't ever find out what you think when you've heard yourself say it?
A: I would like to. I would like to. I'd like to say I'm going instead of I'm coming. I'd like to call out the wrong woman's name.

I'll tell you this. I didn't even surprise myself when I was captured the first time and put in a nuthouse. I must've been about sixteen, seventeen. I was as gone as I think I'm going to get, but nothing I did really surprised me, and I ended up thinking it was just more theater. I ended up thinking even the craziness was feigned and what got me locked up in manacles and chains in Florida and kept on bread and water for two weeks and that kind of thing, in serious lockup, I think it was all an act. I don't think I surprised myself with anything. I think I was pretending. I think I've been pretending for as long as I can remember.

Nothing I say to you, as much as I would like to give it the appearance of vehemence and immediacy, has surprised me. I may be completely transparent to others, and you may be sitting and surmising what I'm up to, maybe saying, I can read this guy through and through, and how come he can't read these conclusions that I come to, but I don't know that I'm escaping. I don't know that I'm ever going to elude the surmise or elude the capture as it were. I can't speak to that. It's not within my power to know, but I get the sense, that's all I require, that, "Gee, I got through with that." I got through with that without making a shambles of things, without delivering myself up to some kind of deep, deep, deep shame, or I pre-empted the shame. I pre-empted the moment. I delivered myself to shame before that person could deliver me to shame, before that person could say, "Hey, you don't make it. You're not in yet." Before that person could say, "Are you there?" I said, "I'm probably not there." So that suffices for me.

I suppose, with how I'm read, both on the page and how I'm read as an editor, and how I'm read as a publisher, and how I'm read as a teacher, the surmise that I think that I've, in an approximate kind of way, produced for you today, isn't the surmise that's mainly made about me. I'm willing to take the rap for what I think my crimes have been, and I think I certainly have committed crimes, but I'm not infrequently, I think rather more to the point, as paranoiacally as I can, the view of me that's posited as the authoritative view, the thing just doesn't square with reality at all. And I don't think it's got by people that have ever had any kind of touch with me at all.

Q: But you like your reputation.
A: I've got to like it. It's what I'm stuck with.

Q: You don't have to like it.
A: I've come to like it. I've come to like it, I suppose. I've even come to like the price I've paid for it.

Q: Let me see if I can steer you back by using a different course. You would never hand over *Chinese* and allow me to edit it.
A: No, I wouldn't. You got me, man.

Q: But these words now are your words and, in a sense, I will be editing you. What's the difference?
A: What's the difference? What is the difference? First-rate question, first-rate question because I wouldn't cede to you, or anyone else, the authority to revise *Chinese* or any of my work. I won't even let you look at it. I don't even want you to fucking look at the goddamn thing until I fix it. I write all kinds of insane letters trying to govern the ungovernable. My god, man, please, please, I'm only giving this to you now in case the plane goes down. I don't even want that record in place because I have my pride, my pride and my vanity.

Well, gee Rob, I don't know that it's going to be possible for me to answer it with any adroitness. You've got me captured.

Probably because my valorizing of this episode in speech is very different from my valorizing of the other. That's plain to see. I don't know what you're going to make of this, this exchange between us, but whatever you make out of it, the very best you can make out of it, it will have been a collaborative effort.

Q: Does the fact that this is a collaboration absolve you of a certain responsibility?
A: That's it. That's the word. That's the word. That's the word, man. That's the word. See, I wrote about twenty books before *Capote*, under other names, and as long as it was under another name I didn't give a shit what I'd done, what kinds of errors might be in place. I never have looked back. And I did a lot of work under other people's names, too, when they got fame for it, a lot of fame for it, and I, even in those instances, and there's one instance in which I don't think I couldn't conceivably have labored with a more finely grained tooth comb, that's the expression, with more fine-grained attention than I did. We were revising and revising and revising it over and over again for each edition, taking such pains with every utterance that came out of my mouth in that writer's name. I, nevertheless, am willing to say, although I have acknowledged that I could not edit myself as successfully as I could edit somebody else, or revise myself as successfully as I could revise somebody else, that unless my marriage to the inviolate center of myself as it comes into play by reason of my written utterance, that's to be in touch with the only God I'm ever in touch with. It's the only thing, in all of my experience, that's even prospectively sacred.

Q: But there's a sanctity that you bestow on the printed word, and in the case of at least two of your works, soon to be all of your works, the printed word changes. I guess what I'm asking for is ungivable, even if you have the desire.

You've published dick books and brain books, but the separation seems to be caused only by time. Why is *Epigraph*, after twenty-nine tries, still a dick book? When does it become a brain book? When did *Capote* become a brain book?
A: Time's the big fucker, man, and these designations we're offering as if they are polarities, dick and brain, really aren't, as both of us know.

Q: Is time the only thing that can provide the distance?
A: No, no. I don't think so. I think intellect has got a lot to do with it. There are some people who are smart. If I were to speak of my friends, DeLillo and Ozick, they're both really fucking smart, really smart, you know. I would never make this claim. I'm always prepared to argue with my students that smarts has nothing to do with it. That the mind can, in fact, be in your way, but as I measure, after the fact, my life, because I see my life after the fact now, those persons that have done noble and real work with respect to the page, given that polarity that has been invoked, dick books and mind books, they're all smart. The ones I have named are really fucking smart. They're sure as hell smarter than I am. I don't like having to concede that. I would rather think that cleverness, I would rather think that devotion would do, stamina would do, that desire would do. I don't want to be seen as good and smart. I'd rather be seen as the supreme swindler. I'd rather be seen as the grand artificer.

Q: Then you've pretty much got what you want, haven't you?
A: Well, you're very genial to offer that observation. From your mouth to God's ears, even though God doesn't exist for me, Rob. You make me grin. But I don't, really. You see, the people I named, they could get that thing down that I told you I couldn't get down. They could get anything down. As I read through DeLillo's *Underworld,* I came again and again to the altogether unpleasant recognition that this guy can do things I can't even imagine getting words around.

There's a moment in this book when he's writing about the major dump out on Staten Island, and it's just a bit. I remember it exactly in the manuscript because I was reading the thing and I said, "I'm not going to call." I'm not going to call him until I finish the whole damn thing, you know. It was deep in where he's offering you up the behavior of some seagulls over the dump as they are suddenly fastened in the air and he follows the word, "regardful, ready to fly."

Now, I couldn't do that. First of all, I couldn't look at seagulls moving anywhere, in any circumstance, even imagined seagulls, and render them. I couldn't give you the sense of a seagull, and I couldn't give you that sense of a seagull as it comes to its pause and then begins to fly again with the word "regardful." The kind of looking about that one sees in the seagull's behavior. That word "regardful" would never ever be rendered to me. I could seek its deliverance the rest of my days and would never get it because I could never study the object with the form of attention required to produce the word "regardful" from it. I could never get it.

That's not a matter of character because I've got character in spades, I think I do. I'm not chicken shit. I've never walked away from a fight. I'm willing to stand up to any fucking thing, really man, I am, to be killed on it. I believe in the writing of a book as signing your own death warrant. That's how it should be if it's to be a proper book. But DeLillo can get that "regardful" because I think he's got an intellectual power. He's got mind in amplitude I'm never going to have. I can say the same about certain other parties including McCarthy. And I feel so damned deprived on account of it.

I used to pal around with James D. Watson, the double helix guy, and I've known one or two really pretty smart cookies in my life, and it's okay to be around Watson, or people like Bloom. There are people like Bloom who can start reciting all of *Murphy* to you, backwards. Bloom can recite all of *Murphy* to you. I mean, you want Beckett? Bloom can give it to you out of his head. I've never seen a mind work faster than James D. Watson's mind. Or Neal Cassady. Cassady could talk around seven different things at the same time and give each one its due. One's a scientist, one's a critic, and one's just a guy on the street, you know, but DeLillo and Ozick and Brodkey. These are unforgivable. They're writers and they bring to the task of writing an amplitude of intellect.

Q: Don't you have an appreciation for them, as writers, if for no other reason than that they can do things that you can't as a writer?
A: They should be there as my models, as what I posit as the heroic, because I'm of the same category. Is that what you're saying?

Q: No, only if you need to render a seagull should you hold them up as models.
A: But I don't need to render a seagull. Who needs a seagull? I want to write about what's in my heart and what's inside me. I don't want a seagull. Seagulls are in the world. Anybody can look at it. Anybody could look at it, but you see, he could've looked at my shit, any of those persons named

could've looked at my shit, whatever my interior shit is, and rendered it. You see, that's the thing. They could do a better job. They could deliver that moment, that glance that I took, that peek I had, when I looked on the unpeekable, the unlookable, when I looked at Barbara Lish when she was in that condition, in that circumstance I described to you, and they would get it out. They would get all of it.

Q: No. They can't be more Gordon Lish than Gordon Lish.
A: I would like to think they wouldn't have seen it in the first place. I would like to think they would've seen something an instant later, an instant before, and not seen the very thing that I saw.

Q: Because you want that moment for yourself.
A: That's right. That's right.

Q: Didn't you remark that *Epigraph* was a book of a man driven insane by grief? Or am I misquoting?
A: I don't have a problem with that. Is he driven insane by grief? He's ultimately a swindler. I'll stay with that.

Q: He's a swindler early on.
A: He ends up a swindler. He seems to become more and more revealed as he speaks. He seems to have removed a certain number of veils, but I think he remains quite wonderfully clothed. He's shrewd to the end. But I don't think I can even read it now. The only true thing in that book, the only true thing in that book, honest to Pete, Rob, I didn't even say, and that's Nietzsche at the very end of it. That's the only true damn thing in there, and that's the last page of the book.

Q: There seems to be a falling off though, and calling him ultimately a swindler suggests that the man is in control. Don't you have to be in control to be a swindler? The narrator of *Epigraph* comes apart in the same way as the narrator of *Dear Mr. Capote* comes apart, but in *Epigraph* it's a contrivance?
A: Yes. Don't you think that control is false? That the equivalency between control and fraudulence is apt? What you want, we're talking now about the other, saying, not with a withering measure, "Are you in yet?" We want the other, driven quite beside herself in fulfillment of what it is that's being offered, so that one wants the reader somehow beside himself in response to one's manipulations but one is forever manipulating.

One's probably never going to be in enough, probably isn't even in to begin with, is always trying to develop the apparition of being in, the appearance of being in, putting something in the place of what, if you put it in, you may never be able to bring back out again.

I'm a guy who could get in a car with Cassady and drive like a lunatic, but get to the destination. Some people get in the car and they don't ever get out. You know what I'm saying? I want to get where I'm going. I don't want to lose myself along the way. I haven't gotten lost yet and I'm almost sixty-three. I understand the authority of that exaltation—let's get lost. I understand the beauty of that, the exorbitance of that. I would posit this as the sublime for all of my students, but would I ever take myself there into it? No, no. I want to get there.

Q: So the narrator of *Epigraph* doesn't lose his way? The narrator of *Epigraph* is as much in control at the end of the novel as he is at the beginning?
A: Yes, absolutely.

Q: What about the narrator of *Dear Mr. Capote*?
A: Ditto, ditto. You know, the narrator being myself. I mean, after all, I'm Davie.

Q: But don't you need a separation between narrator and author?
A: If I offer the separation then yes, he lost himself more, he loses himself more. You know, *Peru* ends with that kind of moment, that moment when he's seeking escape from all of this and calls out about the cab driver and all of that. Though you may have seen a very bad version of that thing. It pains me. That novel, it seems to me, as I read it now, seems to be a very homosexual novel. That seems to me to be really altogether about that, about the speaker's falling into the colored man, falling into the taxi driver. I think it's all really about that. As I read the book now it seems to be quite absolutely about these matters, but he nevertheless remembers, you know, his father's telephone number. He's able to produce his father's telephone number. He hasn't forgotten.

See? This would be very like the revision I want to insist upon. I'm going to get it back for another run through because I see now that the number comes up twice. I must've inserted that when I did the paperback version of it because the number wasn't there at all in the original version, I do believe. It only comes up in the very end, so now the right number comes up twice before: Lackawanna 4–1810. The last time the number appears, it ought to be wrong and I can still catch that. It ought to be wrong.

Q: So *Peru*'s not rewritten yet?
A: Not yet. I just got it from the exchange we had right now. I have revised it, but I'm waiting for the third pass to come back to me, and by Christ, the last time that number is uttered it ought to be wrong. It ought to be wrong. Shit, I got to make two changes in that thing because I also want to add a name to the dedication. I've fallen in love, you see.

Q: But now you've proven yourself wrong because you said you never surprise yourself.
A: Yes, I just did now. But you furnished the occasion for it. I never would've thought of it had we not been talking. You're my editor. I never would've had the idea.

Q: I don't want to equate *Peru*, and *Epigraph*, and *Dear Mr. Capote* with Faulkner's *As I Lay Dying*, but in that novel Darl loses control, and he is, in effect, the narrator of that book.
A: I tried to read that book recently, about a summer ago.

Q: The circumstances are not dissimilar. Granted, there are more voices, but the progression is similar and Darl does lose his sanity by the end. He loses control. He's no longer being manipulative. In my mind, he loses control of his rational being when his family turns on him at the graveyard and sends him off to the asylum. They get rid of him to save the money for the burned barn, and it's that betrayal that causes him to lose control, but you're telling me that the narrator of *Peru* and the narrator of *Epigraph* and the narrator of *Dear Mr. Capote* are still as in control at the end of those novels as they are at the beginning, and so therefore they do not have that moment of loss that Darl experiences.
A: They are because I am. They are because I am. And I've tried to get rid of my mind.

Q: I'm really surprised that you don't insist on more separation between author and character.
A: I'd be a fraud.

Q: How is that different from putting the words "a novel" on the title page?
A: None of this, really, is reportable fact. My God, none of this is reportable fact. Certainly I'm making no effort at all in the reading of these things, after the point of composition, in the reading of them, to find some kind of moral

plan different for myself than I would find for the narrator. I mean, I'm prepared to answer for the narrator as if I were.

I recall a time when Bellow was asked about Augie March in relation to Reaganomics. He was asked the question in some interview, How would Augie March behave during the Reagan period in relation to Reaganomics? And he made a reply as if what was ink on paper somehow existed as an authentic being that would have an authentically statable response to conditions. I thought nothing could be more preposterous, nothing could be more ridiculous, but I didn't invent Augie March. I only invented a version of Gordon Lish, and I can tell you exactly how Gordon Lish would feel in any circumstance, and I don't want to make the claim that there's any kind of distance, any real distance, any statable distance, between myself and the name I'm using for myself in my books.

Q: But you see the problem I have. I don't see how claiming a separation between author and narrator is any more fraudulent than putting the words "a novel" on the title page in order to present it as a work of fiction.
A: There are certain frauds one is more comfortable with than others. I think it was becoming sort of modish not to make a designation of any kind when I started to put out these books. Is it still in the mode? I don't know. I know in 1984 with *Capote* I had the sense that it was getting to be modish to leave off a designation, and I always work against the mode, whatever the mode is.

Q: Were all previous twenty-eight versions of *Epigraph*—even though no others were epistolary—what could be described as a type of monologue?
A: Yes. Oh, absolutely. That would be true. That would be true.

Q: Is the monologue a congenial form?
A: You're discovering my only form, I think. It better be congenial.

Q: Are you capable of writing another type of novel?
A: Oh, I have, under other names. A standard kind of novel? Third person and all that?

Q: Yes, in another point of view. At this moment.
A: Oh, now? Under my own name? I wouldn't in a million years. Wouldn't in a million years. The only novel I've got under my own name that presumably

doesn't have me as a fixture in it is the novel *Extravaganza*, which I will presently revise, I suppose. But that novel's just a stunt. It's a bunch of jokes.

But I don't think I could, Rob. I've started several just as Cynthia Ozick has lately started a book in the first person and has some misgivings about a book in the first person. I would start a book in some other point of view. There are many, many points of view aside from the ones routinely cited. There are all kinds of ways of producing once removed and once removed. There are all kinds of tricks, but the only point I want to make is that I rather imagine that, in due course, I would think better of it, having made my way into the text feeling that somehow I was hobbling myself and that it's not worth the hobbling. Just to be able to point to a book that was rendered by reason of another kind of device wouldn't be worth the price of not getting far enough in.

Q: So it's a moot question. It doesn't matter whether the monologue is a congenial form. It's your form.
A: I'm my object. I'm my character. I've got no other. I don't believe in any other.

Self-Interview

Gordon Lish / 1996

"Self-Interview" by Gordon List was first published in *Creative Nonfiction* issue #5 and appears here by permission of the Creative Nonfiction Foundation.

Editor's note: According to the author, a reporter from Interview Magazine *initially interviewed Gordon Lish for an article. Evidently,* Interview *was unsatisfied; it subsequently sent Lish a list of questions, asking him to make the interview "more accessible"; this "Self-Interview" was the result.*

This is a setup, right? It's all a setup, right? I mean, I am not sitting somewhere shooting my mouth off to somebody sitting the same somewhere with me. There is no tape-recording going on. There is no note-taking going on. What the deal is instead is that I, Lish, am sitting by my lonesome with a list, which list is the product not of my contrivance but of *Interview*'s. (How else have the composure to manage the acoustical divertissement of *list* and *Lish* whilst evincing seeming indifference to an exhibition of an absence of humility?) I mean, the entries that constitute it, this list, *Interview* entered them. Fine. I'm ready. Got pencil and paper. Actually, it's a lie—got felt-tip and paper. Anyway, here is the list as *Interview* made it—Death and Immortality, the Most Overrated Writers in America, Harold Brodkey, Harold Bloom, My Being Called the Antichrist, Knopf, What Writing Means to Me, What My Enemies Mean to Me, and, finally, me, Gordon Lish. Hey, that's me again—Lish again! Swell. Here goes. *Death?* Scared shitless of it. Not of dying—which I elect to accuse of being sexy and dramatic and an occasion for rapturous opportunism and for a certain ultimacy in narcissism—but of being dead. Which state of non-being, reported allure of consciouslessness notwithstanding, I would do anything to get out of. Even art. Like remarking, for example, the hallucination written into the gerund just used: because you're not going to, I'm not going to, no one's going to, be anything. So to say *being dead* is to get it wrong because you're saying it wrong. And ditto, less tellingly but tellingly enough, goes for saying *non-being,* fair enough? So by my *saying* speech says it wrong, I can believe myself to be in charge of the conditions, which is indeed an illusion, but, I claim, not an unprofitable one. Skip it, it goes without saying I am not in charge of anything by saying. But I give myself to believe that I sort of maybe tragically magically pretty pathetically pitiably a little am—by placing into motion a spoken token of myself, a meagreness, yes, but one whose dialectical action I can pretend transmutes me, its origin, into a muchness by reason (irrational reason) of my being the father of it, okay? Doing art is not a way of saying it right but of saying it as wrong you can say it—namely, an act of saying under the sign of your hallucination, not under anyone else's. Which is why the other famous faith system we devised for ourselves doesn't do a job for me. Likelier for me to get myself to think I can overcome, or can march myself to a distance from, Beckett's sign than God's. God's sign—the event of my end, that unimpeachable dissolution—is very dense and specific. Whereas Beckett's transgression against me, his text, is nowhere near as material and aggressive. I wake up innocent but hours nearer my undoing. This is an offense God delivers to me—Jesus, Jesus!—in irrepressibly vivacious and precise detail. Everything else in experience (we can take Beckett again, or take *pease porridge hot, pease porridge cold,* or take the mortification of the flesh) is comparatively soft and insubstantial and thus more or less resistible, yes? God—God's agent nature—is the one object whose incommensurate power nothing I can do can subdue. Oh, fiddlesticks. Give me Beckett—and the other mighty dead—that I may be among them or even trick myself to believe that I am over them. Give me—guess I am quoting Frost—any chance bit that I might manipulate it—am done with the quoting—that I might make of the labor a deformation in my name—the controlled conjunctions, continuities, turbulences, morbid deviations, and so forth. False, false, false, to be sure, but here's a deception I can let myself succumb to because my name is Gordon, is Lish, is language, is not God, is not the clock, is not the rock. Vanity, vanity, vanity—you bet. So, therefore, why not—next-entry-wise—notions of *immortality?* Which all it is is vanity imagining for itself a future, no? Well, immortality, yes, such a notion is right up there with the other enabling fictions—those of no fear, no severance, unbreachable sovereignty, anxiety-free freedom, perfection, completion. It couldn't hurt. It could only help. Glad to go along with it for the time being. *Most Overrated Writers in America?* You mean writers of fiction of my generation in the context of their fictions? Okay, how about this—how about every writer of fiction but Lish? That's one answer to your question—probably the only unquestionably durable answer the person named Lish could contribute. But here's another—every writer of fiction but the Don DeLillo who wrote any novel Don DeLillo wrote, every writer of fiction but the foregoing and the Cynthia Ozick who wrote "Bloodshed" and "Usurpation: Other People's Stories," every writer of fiction but the foregoing and the Cormac McCarthy who wrote *Outer Dark* and *Blood Meridian*, every writer of fiction but the foregoing and the Harold Brodkey—of course, of course!—who wrote "His Son, in His Arms, in Light, Aloft," who wrote "Verona: A Young Woman Speaks," who wrote "Ceil," who wrote "S. L.," who wrote "Largely an Oral History of My Mother," who wrote "The Boys on Their Bikes." Please, you want for me to badmouth? I am happy to badmouth—both the living and the dead. I could give you names and addresses till the cows come home. But so go pick for yourself. Because whatever proposition you come back to me with, chances are it wouldn't be in me to rumpus around with you on the account of it. Neither, it seems reliable to assert, will it be in history for it to do so. On the other hand, I beg you not ever to come back to me with any of the dozens of, with any of the scores of, with any of the hundreds of grandeurs America underpraises, dispraises, or—the fuckers!—appraises neither one way nor the other. I mean, ignores, is ignorant of, proclaims its smug ignoramusness because of. As witness your *New York Times*, your *Village Voice*, your *New York Review of Books*, to cite certain more notable igginesses in sight. Having not one word to say, the lot of them, either for or against, for instance, Dawn Raffel's "In the Year of Long Division"—or either for or against Sam Michel's "Under the Light," for instance. Ditto Brian Evenson's "Altmann's Tongue," ditto Victoria Redel's "Where the Road Bottoms Out," which forinstancing I guess I could also get myself to keep up until kingdom come. *Harold Brodkey?* We used to be friends. Or we used to appear to be friends. Now we are no longer friends—neither actually nor apparently. *Harold Bloom?* We used to be friends. We used to appear to be friends. Now we are no longer friends—neither actually nor apparently. Ah, but these states of affairs hardly rule out my reading Brodkey and Bloom. You would have to watch me pack up and take myself off to jail if there were a law made that tried to make me quit reading Brodkey and Bloom. Which would just this minute go double for Donoghue and Kristeva and Deleuze and Guattari and Levinas and Lentricchia and Langer and Nelson Goodman and Adorno and—who have I just now got laid out on the tiny table next to my toilet?—Hegel. Hey, hey—how about, what about "Gordo, why come is it that you are no longer friends with Brodkey, for one, and with Bloom, for another?" Answer? Because he's a shit, for one, and a shit, for another! Answer? Because he's a stinking rotten shit, for one, and a stinking rotten shit, for another! But who's calling names? Am I calling names? These men will be among the mighty dead one day—gods, be gods, such as anyone might come gloriously to install either or both for himself. But better revered as ghosts changelessly vaporous in the firmament than spotted as all too fleshly moral dishevelments for the children to see panhandling on the Rialto. *My Being Called the Antichrist?* No kidding. Somebody did that? Who did that? Maybe in Los Angeles maybe. Maybe in Portland. Maybe in Chicago. Here in NYC all I am trying to do is betray, betray—but on the page, baby, on the page!—such that the ties that bind me will be let loose from me for long enough for me to get a toe or two into a thereto untrammeled domain. This means being against everything—against it!—but that means, first and foremost, being against myself. So, check, if there is good in me, then I am against it—but let us seek to keep the categories discrete. I'm all for anything, all for being Yertle the turtle, plus also all for opposing what I say I'm all for—but on the page, baby, on the page! Which happens to be the elsewhere I chose and still choose. Well, okay, I admit it—maybe also, you know, forgive me, don't get excited, but, right, right, no argument, it's true, put the cuffs on me, you got me, I give up—it all goes ditto for in the class, where I am the demon's consort, its thing, its conduit. *Knopf?* We used to be friends. We appeared to be friends. (Come on, you know the rest of the dirge by now.) But so what's the deal here, so friendless at 61? Am I, at long last, wising up? Which, however, it not to say you will catch me looking one inch inattentive to the careers of any of the following Knopf undertakings—Gary Lutz's "Stories in the Worst Way," Jason Schwartz's "A German Picturesque," Diane Williams's "The Stupefaction," Christine Schutt's "Nightwork," Ben Marcus's "The Age of Wire and String," Ken Sparling's "Dad Says He Saw You at the Mall," Anne Carson's "Plainwater"—since it was I who, before my being Knopfed off, took them all on—not to mention, proud to mention, Denis Donoghue's "Walter Pater." Oh, and another thing—Wayne Hogan's "Book of Life"—no, correct that, "Book of Tubes"—be smart and get in touch with me at the Q, at 212-888-4769, if you are a publisher who is not too chickenshit to stand strong for a corker. Now then, "What Writing Means to Me?" Meaning itself. Despite the meaninglessness of it. An answer to the insult. Despite the exorbitance of it. The works, or Works, which was my dead wife's name before it was Lish. But best to say time. Because time beats meaning. Best to say writing means life lived in Lish-made time, not life spent in given time, not life suffered in death-row time, which is nature's time, dig? "What My Enemies Mean to

Me?" Everything—the works (oh, don't worry, I know all too well, I know exactly what I am saying) again—the inertia-taunting otherness in me—starting with God and with time and with Mommy and Daddy and ending with the vicious incurable ironizing instability of the sentence. Oh, heck—of the comma, of the period. On the other hand, who, what, is there anything exterior or, for that matter, interior, that is not the enemy? That is not an impediment to your existence, to your freedom? "Gordon Lish?" Hey, that's me, that's me!—my name, not the first governance but the most agreeable governance. Well, isn't it, wasn't it, a naming, the whole damned deal, an onomatologically determined act of being? Which, when you get right down to it—which is where we're all going to one day have to get to—namely, right down on your back on your deathbed to it—which would you sooner say? Give you two choices. "Oh, well, that's life." Or: "Yeah, that was me." It of course being conceded there is any say left in you.

An Interview with Gordon Lish

Deron Bauman / 1996

From *elimae*, 'Walt' issue, 1996. © 1996 Deron Bauman. Reprinted by permission.

Deron Bauman: In the epigraph to *Extravaganza,* you state, "the positive is already given." As the reader continues, the power of this statement becomes apparent. Do you think an approach to fiction in which some larger occurrence is alluded to, be it historical, psychological, or emotional, is a valid way to approach all fiction? Should the aim of fiction in general be to touch upon that which cannot fully be said?

Gordon Lish: The epigraph you cite from *Extravaganza* comes from Kafka. It concerns the notion that everything given, that everything, if you will, written, is what the writer who comes after confronts. The writer does not confront a blank for there can be no blank. What he confronts, in that it is given, is the given, is therefore the positive, against which, if he is to do anything at all that is needed at all, he must produce the rebuke—namely, therefore, produce the negative. The completed couplet goes something like this: "It is up to us to accomplish the negative; the positive is already given." To my mind, one ought always to have this Kafkan counsel in mind. Why it seemed to me particularly apt in the instance of *Extravanganza* bears on the novel's aim to bear on the Holocaust—or, rather to say, on writing that has occurred, on report that has occurred, on sensations and sensationalisms already knowably in place in response to this unknowable, unreportable, uncontainable event. To refer to this accumulation with respect to the Kafkan adjuration—that is, as the "positive"—seems to me especially obscene. Yet this is what it is to write with the event in mind—an obscenity. You see the difficulty here. It is inescapable. But, of course, what object, what event, is not, in this light, obscene? Meanwhile, is it not art's nasty task to seek to subdue the difficult? No fiction can render its object, or even an aspect of its object. A fiction renders a fiction, making the making of fictions an inexhaustible activity—a time-passing, safety-making infinitude of evasions, disguises, preenings, swindles, defenses.

Q: It would be easy to assume that making yourself an implied part of the plot structure by creating a character in much of your fiction referred to as Gordon Lish would cause the reader to feel closer to you, but, sometimes, I feel the opposite, as if you introduce this personalized character as a way to draw attention away from yourself, as if pointing into a mirror, saying, "That is the real me."
A: Gordon Lish shows up in much of my writing because Gordon Lish is the writer of my writing. If he is to be thought "Gordon Lish" and not Gordon Lish, a deformation and not myself, then it is the reader who is the clever one for being competent of achieving this scission. Look, Gordon Lish does not show up in my life very much, at least so far as I am able to tell. For him to show up in my fiction, for me to cause Gordon Lish to show up in my fiction, is for me to bless him with manifestations of life of which he would otherwise not be sensible.

Q: There is a point in *My Romance* at which you say, "I am a vain man." The first time I read that sentence I was caught off guard both by its revelation and its humanity. If you allow that the introduction of yourself as a character in much of your fiction is a conscious manipulation of the reader's expectations, can a statement like this be taken at face value?
A: Everything on the page, to the extent that I can manage to make it so—and I must tell you that I fancy myself willing to make every effort to make it so, to let myself recoil from nothing to make it so—is, to quote you, a "conscious manipulation." Oh boy, do I like to manipulate, do I like to be conscious about doing it. In life, I think I sometimes struggle to manipulate, but ordinarily, I think, I must make a botch of it for not keeping my wits—consciousness, consciousness!—enough about me. In fiction, I never quit with trying to pull fast ones. You think I sometimes outwit myself? I think I sometimes outwit myself. Anyway, take nothing I say at face value—not if I say it in a book, anyway. Wallace Stevens calls the writer an actor, the book theater. Me, I'd say that goes for the whole deal—all the way to who took the picture and whom it pictures.

Q: It seems to me in your later novels, *My Romance* and *Zimzum*, there is an homage in the torrent of language your sentences create to Thomas Bernhard. Do you feel an affinity to his work, and if so, how would you characterize the effect of his use of language? Are there any other writers to whom you feel an affinity? Which writers do you consider to be the best of the twentieth century? Do you, like your colleague, Harold Bloom, subscribe to a canon which can be looked upon as a unified continuum of literary history? If so, who are the writers from the breadth whom have been important to you, or, that you simply enjoy?

A: Nope, no admission of sentiments of affinity to Bernhard beyond thinking he was doing good things. But so, in *Blood Meridian*, was McCarthy—great things, great things. It would be paying myself an honor I don't deserve for me to make claim to my having, your word, "an affinity" with either of these fellows. You're asking me to collect to my attention the writers I feel an affinity for, with, to? Gee, I don't even know what adverb applies—or best suits—or is it preposition? Strongest, for my memory, imaginative writers of the twentieth century? Shit, that would be to fashion a list, which didn't DeLillo go to the trouble of telling us is not one of the more attractive of our American hysterias? I'm guilty of enough without looking to go get myself guilty of that one too. Let's leave the list-making to Bloom, H.—and welcome he is to the profiteering and shame to be earned from his folly. On the other hand, hand me Bloom as critic, Donoghue as critic, Kristeva as critic, and I'll hand you a list and a half, fair enough? Further on this score: the naming of names. DeLillo's my friend, Ozick's my friend, Lentricchia's my friend, Donoghue's my friend—my students—not a little number who were, not a little number who are—they're my friends, my friends, and they deliver to my attention sentences I cherish, sentences I venerate, sentences that give me no peace. But to turn over to you names and addresses and not have present among them the name and address of a student who is right this instant turning over the sentence I will cherish the most, will venerate most, will be jostled by most?—never, I'm not talking! But I'll say this to you—they're all Americans, of course, the ones who knock me down and run away with my heart and my lungs and my liver. I grew up reading the Italians and the Hispanics here and there and the Germans and the French—but it was a fool who believed he was doing reading.

Q: Of the writers you have published, who do you consider to have gone on to create authentic careers?
A: This next question calls for list-making again. Nuts to it.

Q: Is there any writer you feel, as Bloom would put it, you need to conquer?
A: Yeah, Bloom, I need to conquer, kick the crap out of, Bloom. In the Bloomian sense, of course. Finally, it would seem to stand too distant from probity for me to fail somewhere—here, then—to cite Brodkey, which is to

say, the Brodkey of, and solely the Brodkey of, certain short fictions, these being "Largely an Oral History of My Mother," "His Son, in His Arms, in Light, Aloft," "Ceil," "Verona: A Young Woman Speaks," and "S. L." and perhaps the title story of the collection these fictions are to be found in—*Stories in an Almost Classical Mode*. Well, Brodkey conquered, kicked the crap out of, himself—and handily enough for all concerned.

Q: With the amount of writing you receive, is it possible for you to help a writer find the core of his or her story, or do they have to be on target before they submit to you?
A: Don't know that one wants to "help a writer find the core of his story," but I don't think it's not in the cards for an editor/teacher to so assist, in any event. There might be readier means to bring the work to itself. That "core" you're directing attention to, isn't actually. We have come to a matter rich in perplexity, congestion of appearances and disappearances. Let me refer your attention to any reliable text in psychoanalytic practice. Do I imagine the editor/teacher might be imagined as such a practitioner? Well, he might. As respects my own practices, however, they're rather closer in character, I expect, to the dexterities of the Visigoth.

Q: Being known mostly as an editor of fiction, how do you approach the poetry that is sent to you, or the collections that you publish? Do you consider poetry to be on the artistic level with prose?
A: I come to poetry no differently from how I come to prose. Too, I can't see any reason to ask for a distinction between the values of these artifacts—their effects, their forces. It may be said—and I would say it at a shout—that there is, of what one sees that's being done, as little to get excited about either in the one or in the other. There is much that is merely there—somewhere, anywhere. There is the teensiest bit that is there and that is nowhere else but there and that makes certain its domain is the imperium. But, let's face it, that teensiest bit comes to a copia enough for all.

Q: Is there a sentence or paragraph you admire most?
A: Crazy—a sentence, a paragraph I most admire. I imagine I do this thing you find me doing—that I write, that I teach writing, that I edit writing—because there was such a bounty of sentences, of paragraphs, that I so much admired.

Q: In the early part of the century, Alfred Stieglitz set the tone for American modern art with the publication of his magazine *Camera Work* and the

showing of artists such as Picasso, O'Keefe, and Matisse in his 291 Gallery. Would you indulge this analogy as far as it might extend to you?
A: You're asking for a list again—or, more adroitly, for exhibition. Please, those whose work I brought out while I was at *Esquire*, while I was at Knopf, not to mention then and now in *The Quarterly*, these persons must suffice in their totality, I suppose. Do you insist I say Gary Lutz, Jason Schwartz, Diane Williams, Dawn Raffel, Noy Holland, Sam Michel, Christine Schutt, Victoria Redel, Brian Evenson? Whoops! Hey, these are my students! And what about Michael Kimball? Oh, you see, you see?—it's atrocious—I will not do it. No, tell you what—I *will* do it, as Stieglitz did. Give me an exhibition space, give me a publishing company—come on, you airwave people, I dare you, give me one!

Q: In the seventies and eighties, Raymond Carver was upheld as a master of storytelling and form. Due to this, many young writers began to emulate him. During the eighties and nineties, it seems your magazine, *The Quarterly*, has taken over this role. Regardless of your feelings for or against Carver, how would you gauge the impact of *The Quarterly*?
A: How could I state the uses *The Quarterly* sponsors for the national literature? I do my best with it, *The Q*. Dana Spiotta does her best with it. Jodi Davis does her best with it. We're doing our best with it. May it happen that our best with it will inure to some good for it, migrating pronominal reference intended, pal.

(With regard to the short-story writer whose name you remarked, the matter is a tale unto itself. This setting is scarcely the one wherein that tale might, with any sufficiency, be told. Will it be told? Oh, I think so, I think so.)

Q: Who would you consider to be your peers?
A: I don't have peers. My kids had peers. They had them at school, in school, or so it was argued by educationists of the time. I've got some friends—some very, very, very few friends. I gave you the names of three of them. There used to be Bloom, there used to be Brodkey, there used to be even James D. Watson even. Now there's only DeLillo and Ozick and Lentricchia and a couple of others—one writes, one doesn't. Anyway, they're all, the gang of them, peerless, I tell you, peerless in their putting up with me and my me-ness.

Q: In the first pages of *My Romance* and the "Sentences" section of *Zimzum*, there seems to be a lot of sadness concerning your wife. Are the details surrounding this too personal to discuss?

A: There is a novel coming—in the fall of 1996. I'm calling it *Epigraph*. I was not unmindful, when this was the title I chose, that "epitaph" would suggest itself along with other readings of the word. At all events, I make this reply to your interrogative treating my dying wife Barbara, my dead wife Barbara. I mean the book, that fiction, will make my reply to you. But you say sadness. . . . Aren't we always, all of us, for all the hours we can remember, weren't we always, won't we be, won't we be, more and more so—sad, mainly sadnesses, surprising to ourselves when, with embarrassment, coming to notice ourselves not sad, not so, not thus?

Q: With the amount of time you spend teaching, publishing, and writing, do you ever get tired of words? Of these, which do you most enjoy, or, feel is the most important?
A: Tired of words? Crikies, Deron Bauman, I'm scared shitless of words. Hey, look at this one—saloogi, saloogi. How can a feller get tired of anything as vicious and awful as that? Jabes asserts, and I'm glad he does, that for you to obey the word is for you to proceed murder by murder. So say it's Gordon Lish—or is it "Gordon Lish"—and a sort of kill-or-be-killed condition between him, or "him," and that one, that word, the word saloogi. Well, maybe it was spelled—if anybody who ever did it to somebody, ever "played" it, ever spelled it—salugi or even saloojee—and maybe there was even a capital S on it for the orthography to come out right pursuant to it. It was, anyway, meanwhile—"Hey, Gordie! Hey Gordie! Salugi, salugi!"—a matter of life or death. I grant you, a person can get tired—I've seen this, I've been pressed into instruction in it—even of a matter of life or death—but there's fear in me still—and, as a result, interest. A deal more of it than there is in me for anything else, I bet you—fragment that this last of this was.

Q: The process of writing, revising, and editing allows a person a good amount of time to say what he wants to say, in a way he wants to say it. Do writers in general, or you in particular, use this as a way to combat the immediacy, or at times, the relentlessness, of living?
A: Your final question is the question. It was, however, answered all along the way, wasn't it? One contrives an hallucination, confects for oneself a made hallucination in order to distract oneself from the given hallucination. So this brings us back to Howth, no? I mean to the counsel Kafka would have wished for us to consider at the start of this—reversing the charge, inaugurating a negative from a positive, displacing the given with the made. Like, you know, it's employment, baby—whereas these times, *any* times, aren't they hard times?

Molly Bloome Talks with Gordon Lish

Molly Bloome / 2002

From *Taint Magazine,* February 2002. © 2002 Taint Magazine. Reprinted by permission.

Gordon Lish: Okay, ready to go.
Molly Bloome: Okay, tell me about the women.
GL: The women, they began with my mother.

MB: No, that doesn't count; that's a given.
GL: Is it a given?

MB: No, go ahead. You can go back to your mother.
GL: It is a given, you are alleging, that one's sexual proclivity—or shall we say, vector or energy—derives from a parent, and affection for a parent, a dependency on a parent, which focuses the body on that parent? I don't know if I accept that view, but let's say I have been, all my life, in pursuit of my mother, so that any women I might chat with you about would be measured against that format.

MB: Standard maybe.
GL: Standard, format, mold.

MB: Prototype.
GL: Paradigm, paragon.

MB: Archetype.
GL: Epigene, epitome, epigone—however it's said. The woman would succeed or fail in my affections relative to her measure against this prototype, which is understood in absolutist terms.

MB: Absolutely.
GL: Right, there is a theory in psychoanalysis about good mother-bad mother that—

MB: No, this mother is your mother.
GL: In this context, it is the ideal mother.

MB: Your ideal mother. That's all we care about here.
GL: Right, the individual's ideal mother, the male individual, or whatever person of whatever sexuality interested in women. In lieu of being interested in—I think your position was the sentient event, my having exchanged the kind of devotion I have to the formation of utterance, for the formation of a kind of sensation, unique to the interplay, or finely put, copulation, between a man and a woman.

MB: What do you mean by sensation?
GL: By sensation, I mean that feeling, which seems to derive both from the body and the mind, or, one might claim, in this combination, the soul.

MB: How would you say that relates to perception?
GL: It's all perception. It is all perception.

MB: Some philosophers would say that isn't true.
GL: If the object remains exterior to yourself, there is no way to apprehend it, save that you perceive it. The perception is, doubtless, to produce itself at an extreme deformation from the reality, the objectivity, but, nevertheless, one is hopeless in his quest to ever make any distance between himself and his perception.

MB: Epicurus said—
GL: Epicurus. Is this some fucking dead man you're—

MB: Epicurus said sense perception is the source of all knowledge.
GL: Sense perception is all knowledge.

MB: The source of.
GL: The source of all knowledge.

MB: What do you think of that?
GL: I like that. It seems to coincide with my notions about what Alphonso Lingis is saying—that we are in the world in relation to the way our body aligns

with the world. I suppose he means by that, all of the abilities of our body to appropriate the world for our senses. So I would go along with it, lady.

MB: So do you think our bodies determine what we perceive, what is felt?
GL: Sure, where the body is turned, what the body is willing to apprehend, what the body is willing to, first, before perceive, receive. It's like Kesey used to claim: If I didn't believe it, I never would have seen it. So one has to allow for a certain kind of mental relation with exteriority before one is even in the position to perform the appropriate, or the necessary, or the inexorable deformation.

MB: Go back to the women.
GL: I like to go back to the women. I have a great interest in women.

MB: Starting with your mother.
GL: Starting with my mother, of course, and we might argue that cynosure—understood as the epigone, or the epitome—was followed by a similar feeling, or a feeling that would form the same category, by one for my sister, which I would wonder sometimes is it the case or not. I haven't really quite decided. There was a time when I was seeing, I did believe, in all the women I was consorting with, the same face.

MB: No longer?
GL: No longer, I don't think I do it any longer. There are occasions when it will occur, but fleetingly, not for any lasting time. The duration of this hallucination is rather fleeting.

MB: What about the face? Whose face was it?
GL: Well, that's it. I wanted to know. When I—I think the expression is—racked my brain, in every context, I wanted to see if I were able to conjure up the identity of that face because I knew it to be not the face of a woman in general, but of a specific woman. Maybe it was a familiar face. It proved that I did, for a while, believe after rather a lot of exertion on this score that it was my sister's face, oddly. I first thought it was the face of a former student of mine. Then I got to believe that it was the face of my sister, which is a face that would have affected me forty, fifty years before the student came along.

MB: When that thought occurred to you, did the face go away?
GL: Now, well, that's interesting. That's a very good question because I think for a time the hallucination persisted in precisely the character that

I've described. It was that specific student's face or that specific face of my sister, which was succeeded by the first perception, or deduction—or what else would one call it—or error, let's say error, the first error.

MB: But the face appeared on the women you were making love to?
GL: It became their face. It became the woman's face.

MB: Each woman, every woman.
GL: Yes, and it would appear, sometimes, it would seem, for rather considerable lengths of time. It was rather a protracted misperception.

MB: Give me some of the qualities. Give me the shapes, colors.
GL: The coloring was darker than my mother's hair.

MB: What color was your mother's hair?
GL: My mother's hair was very blonde, and my sister had, I guess what would be called in those days, light brown hair. But the woman's face was notably crowned by hair, hair of a medium length, medium-to-longish length, and it was light brown. The face was longish, I do believe. If you'd ask me was my mother's face longish, or my sister's face longish, I couldn't answer. It haunts me now that I speak with you of this. I have some sense of the verticality, of the vertical axis of that face, but I couldn't produce, at my scant age of sixty-eight, a sense of the verticality versus the longitudinality versus the laterality of my sister's or my mother's face.

MB: What about symmetry?
GL: No, it was somewhat awry. The eyes were close-set. The face was not a symmetrical face, as I recall, but it was the most alluring face I have ever in all my life encountered. It seemed the only face. At first, I thought it was the face of my wife, Barbara, but it happens that Barbara's coloring was very fair. She also was a blonde, as my mother was, and blue-eyed, and this is not a blue-eyed woman. This is a woman whose eyes would be the color I imagine that my sister's eyes were, something like hazel. I think that was a word she used with great pride—not brown, but hazel—because my father had said his eyes were hazel, and my sister, I had the sense, wanted to confirm her relation with my father. I was a bit suspicious of that description, hazel, but I was, of course, too young to know what hazel really was. I still don't know, in fact, what hazel really is.

MB: When did the face first appear? Do you remember?
GL: Yes, I do. It was after my wife was deceased. My wife has been deceased since 1994—about eight years now—and I would see this hallucination having started to occur about four years ago.

MB: And ended, when, months ago?
GL: No, I would say it still persists, from time to time. I have the same—I've taken to calling it—hallucination, but I wonder if that's entirely fair, because it may be that the woman before me, already has in her face certain lineaments that are susceptible to being composed into the face I have in mind. It may be that I'm not beginning with a face that would refuse this kind of deformation. It may have been, to begin with, a face that was susceptible of undergoing this misprision. I could misread this face to make it the face I wanted to read it as.

MB: Does a certain type of woman attract you?
GL: No. Do you mean in my normal comings and goings?

MB: I mean with all the women in your life.
GL: No, because the hallucination I've been referring to occurs only in the course of sexual contact. I would not be sitting with a woman or dining with a woman and suddenly be visited with this transfixing effect in my regard, a face reminiscent of some kind of ur-face, some kind of ur-female face, or female ur-face. I can offer up no measurements, no descriptions of this disablement that seem consistent with any kind of explanation. It didn't happen immediately after my wife died; it happened four years later, that sort of thing.

MB: Right. Yes, I understand completely. (pause) Would any of this have been in *Mysterium*?
GL: You said you understand completely. I hope that's true.

MB: I do.
GL: I do hope that's true.

MB: I do, absolutely, because I don't think there's an exact start point or end point to these sorts of things.
GL: Would any of this have been in *Mysterium?* You've asked a very good question. I don't know, but I do know today, in thinking about returning

to my confection, *Farmingdale*, which is hardly any confection yet—about sixty-five pages of horsing around, but consecutive horsing around. But in thinking about it today, I did make two notes which I think were cribbed from *Mysterium*, and one had to do with reading lettuce.

MB: Reading lettuce?
GL: Well, I can't get into it. I don't want to be too informative. No, no, no, no, no, no.

MB: All right, scratch that.
GL: But two things I've been recalling from *Mysterium* that I thought I might incorporate into *Farmingdale*, or think about incorporating into *Farmingdale*, and one of them bore on the question you've just asked. (pause) I'm not able to remember your question.

MB: The face.
GL: The face, would any reference to that have appeared in *Mysterium*? Well, in *Mysterium*, which I have not really read, you know, I wrote it about three years ago and the publisher held onto it for about two years. I saw the galleys only just recently, and have decided on the basis of my reading of those galleys, up to page fifty-six, to annul the book. I didn't really read beyond page fifty-six, so I've no very clear idea. And you'll say: But Gordon, didn't you read the novel when you wrote the novel? But in a way, I didn't. I really did not. And I certainly didn't read it, as the master, when I had finished it, no, not en toto as I might have done ten years ago. So I have no idea, no idea, really, what's really in the book, though I'm sure that I would like to be enunciated somewhere, because I feel it probably bespeaks one of the truer things about me. And I like to tell the truth. I think it's one of the true things about me, this deformation that I seem to be practicing on a susceptible array of (pause) features before me.

MB: With respect to the face of a woman?
GL: But certain things are always insistent. The hair is always long, for example. It might be interesting to behold; would I see the same woman, yet again, with her hair in a Dutch bob, say? I'll have to think on that. I'll have to look forward to any act of fornication with a woman with her hair cut in a Dutch bob.

MB: You'll let me know? Get back to me on that.
GL: I can only hope that I'll be able to, that I'll have such good luck as to meet such a woman.

MB: Now let's go back to what you said.
GL: From a political standpoint, you understand.

MB: Oh, absolutely, but going back to what you were saying about not reading *Mysterium*—so how could you know you wanted to annul the book, since during the writing of *Mysterium* you still wouldn't know it, because you were really not writing it.
GL: I wasn't, no. Are you saying this now in the sense of one cannot put his foot into the river in the same place twice? Are you saying it in that sense?

MB: No.
GL: Are you saying it in the sense of some kind of dislocation of the soul?

MB: Dislocation, detachment.
GL: Yes, sure, this is an impersonation going on. When one writes, in my view, however one has couched the official point of view, one is always dependent upon a certain auctorial perception. Even if one is writing in a less personal manner, one is always really producing an impersonation of a person, in quote "viewing" what is being written. So there is some kind of impersonation always going on, even if there's not—as I hope to make it in my case—a kind of rather aggressive impersonation. I can only try to write the way I speak, for example. I may have been a bad boy and told many a student years before, write as you speak, but I would like to think I only did that if I had found something in this person's speech, oral speech, that was possessed of a singularity, that a style could be acquired from it. But I think it's rather more of an impersonation.

MB: That's an important distinction to make.
GL: I think it's a very important one. I think it is what makes all my writing fraudulent.

MB: But you could say brilliantly fraudulent.
GL: Well, I can't speak to that.

MB: But some would say.
GL: As I think I was telling you, I did indeed do just this. When someone had flattered me recently, for a book that is rarely read—certainly no one's ever bothered to write me a letter saying gee whiz about it, and this was such a letter—I took myself to the book to read, as has been my practice, to a room I have here in my house, where I keep these books, in some sort

of arrangement to indicate how I'd like them revised, if they should ever achieve that—so I might correct them slightly, or proof them briefly. So I read a page from that book, then kept up a certain resolution, I read a page of yet another book, and then I took myself from that room back to another room where I have hidden the only, so far as I believe, copy of *Mysterium*, namely the proofs, and my emendations up to page fifty-six, most of which consist in x-ing's out—crossing out entire pages. But I thought as I came away from it—I read the first sentence, in fact, it was hard to read it through the scribbling and through all the notations that I've made—(pause)—well, this is not so bad.

MB: (laughter)
GL: It's very good. (laughter) You know?

MB: Even read in another room?
GL: Yes, even read in another room, despite the shocking risk taken in changing the milieu.

MB: How about if you took it out of the house and read it in a coffee shop?
GL: I don't think I could handle that. I couldn't handle that. But reading the book in another room didn't seem to put too much stress upon the sustained re-supposition, and so I patted myself on the back a little bit, and I put it down, hid it again, a little less, I think, assiduously than I did the first time. I think I decided to make it a little more susceptible to discovery.

MB: The title of the book is taking on more and more meaning.
GL: That's funny. In no way was that ever intended.

MB: Maybe it was.
GL: No, heavens, no, but I wished I'd stuck with the original title, which was *Delirium*. I remember calling up DeLillo one day and saying, "I think I'm going to call this book *Mysterium*." And he said, "I don't believe it." And I said, "What do you mean?" And he said, "There was a time when I was going to call one of my novels"—I think, in fact, *Ratner's Star*—"*Mysterium*." He never confirmed my suspicion, but I think that was the book he had thought about calling *Mysterium*. And he said, "Oh, that was the title I had thought of years ago. Well, I guess it's yours now." When I killed the book I called him and said, "You can have it back."

MB: You can have your title back.

GL: But I did think, in coming away from that room, that a facsimile—or the proofs, you could say—just shooting the pages page-by-page, with the scratchings all over the place, the pages all crossed and blacked out—I thought maybe that might be a way to make a book. I know it's been done. I'm sure it's been done. But I've always had the aim to do a novel, a book, that remained a book, kept strictly within the parameters of what we tend to think of as books, in the most traditional sense, in the most conventional sense, that nevertheless could produce an effect that was constituted of formal considerations, that proved to (xxxxxxxx) ["Can't do it again. The only creative act I would be prepared to make the revision of would have been a bold-face lie told to my mother," said Lish, in a telephone conversation regarding the questionable word, January 24, 2002—M.B.] and have that practice again, of racking my brain, to find such mechanisms. I'm sure that would be seen as a rather cheap way to approach the act of performance. But I don't think so. I'm determined to do something that nobody has ever done, and that would start with myself.

MB: Here's a question for you. Maybe this will be a better one.
GL: What was wrong with the last question?

MB: You've already—we've already—discussed it.
GL: Oh, so now it's no good.

MB: No, I mean, so we'll go on.
GL: So it's contaminated now.

MB: No, it's not. Nothing is contaminated.
GL: Tainted now, as I think you would like it to be emphasized.

MB: Did you do impersonations for your mother?
GL: Did I do impersonations for my mother? No, but that's very good. I saw an actor last night on television being interviewed and he was doing imitations of other actors that were very, very convincing. I have a friend named George Andreou who is an astonishingly good mimic; he captures the essence of somebody's speech. No, I have none of that. But when I was a boy, do you mean did I impersonate the boy wounded, did I impersonate the boy happy, did I impersonate the boy devoted to his mother, did I impersonate the boy—? I did impersonate the boy devoted to his mother. Yes, I can recall,

particularly—my mother was a great woman in the needle arts—I was seated in some reverential manner before her, while she sewed, or did something with the needle and thread—spangling, sewing beads on dresses, and so on. I do think that I would compose myself in the aspect of a devoted boy. I think I remember feeling that I was making headway with this pose and I was gaining my love object. I do think so. My mother would, from time to time, confirm with some kind of gesture, her approbation. She would smile at me or she would tap me on the head or something, and that would give me the feeling that I, in fact, had been making ground, making headway, in my seduction of her. So I would affect the devoted—I wouldn't say "son," that would be a word far too dangerous and heady for my kind of boy—I would say, "boy." I'm sure my mental figuration—I'm sure I would say it was the disguise of a good boy, not of a good son. Son would also imply certain political considerations, and civic ones, and that would involve, of course, the father as well.

MB: Are you a devoted lover?
GL: I think I am as certainly achieved on that score now, as ever in my life I was. Was I back when I first lost myself into this preoccupation or, what I would like to call, vocation? Was I one then? Yes, I think I was, because I insisted to Fat Shirley that I loved her.

MB: And maybe you did?
GL: I did, at the time, love her. I know that I was absolutely earnest in this assertion because it was made, I believe, subsequent to my having achieved the status of some occupation of her interior space. So it really wasn't said, I think, as a persuasive device, but rather as a kind of commitment, you might call it. I really did exert a great deal of the probity I have, in my first contact of this kind—telling Fat Shirley that I loved her. Of course, one says this kind of thing, I suppose. In this case one would absolutely have to suppose, because I'd never seen Fat Shirley before. She was produced, suddenly, in the room, as somebody that I could achieve my ambition with, so I had no basis to offer a statement of love.

MB: Fat Shirley was the first.
GL: Fat Shirley was the first. Although there was on the beach, in Florida, a girl. I had gone to Florida, at first, for medical purposes, given the psoriasis that I had in such a superlative form, and the belief generally held that sunshine was the best way to treat psoriasis. So I'd gone down there for a year and ran into a woman, a girl, of course—a woman, heavens. I was thirteen or fourteen. I guess she was fourteen-and-a-half, fifteen. I don't

know. I'd been bar mitzvahed, so I know I was older than thirteen, maybe thirteen-and-a-half, is what I was. She had the kind of hair that I think of when I think of Hedy Lamarr, sort of tightly wavy, parted in the middle, and shoulder length. And I was mad for her, completely mad for her, absolutely mad for her. And at a party—she lived there, she was a resident of this part of Florida—she was having a party, she said, for her classmates—

MB: The girl on the beach.
GL: The girl on the beach, exactly, and they played a game called kiss-and-tackle, which made no sense to me because first you tackled and then you kissed, but they called it kiss-and-tackle. I swear. But we had some kind of conjunction; it would be difficult to say if it were actually an act of sexual intercourse, but it certainly seemed to me that it was. I took it as being one and was devoted to her, and have remained so all my life, I think. I could give you her name, but would not.

MB: We can call her the girl on the beach.
GL: The girl-on-the-beach story.

MB: There must have been a lot of the girl-on-the-beach stories.
GL: There have been girls on the beach.

MB: Precipitated, I suppose—
GL: The most interesting girl-on-the-beach story, I thought, would someday form the basis of a book, as I made *Epigraph,* using the perversity mainly in the sense of a kind of indictment of myself, as failing at a critical time. My mother was dying, it was clear, and I had gone to Florida to be at her side. I had done this for a day or so, and, after all, could not really be in Florida without being called forth into the sunlight, thinking it would somehow facilitate the healing of my psoriasis, or at least the disguising of it. So I concocted some alibi, that I had to go out and I would leave my mother with the companion or the nurse for a while. I made my way to the beach, and while on the beach I had an amazing, amazing, amazing experience that one could only have, I suppose, while one's mother is lying in her deathbed.

MB: Dirty Phoebe.
GL: Dirty Phoebe, exactly. Yes, Dirty Phoebe, glistening in the sun, and then the ocean, Dirty Phoebe, exactly, who I took to be some kind of baroness from Austria.

MB: And ended up being?

GL: Ended up being a nice little gal from Georgia. She was with her daughter, who was the kind of woman that would be photographed by *Playboy* magazine, and who was sunning topless. I'd never seen this kind of thing on a public beach. The daughter was sunning herself topless and the mother was wearing a bikini that was partly even more immodest than toplessness itself, bottomless, as well. I concocted some kind of Jamesean intrigue out of this; these persons were European royalty of some kind hiding away in the States and I had made a romance out of this as I lay in my walking shorts, trying to get a bit of sun. I watched and watched and watched. When the older woman went down to the water, I went down to the water as well. We stood in that style that people stand whenever they're trying to affect a pick-up on the beach, or not at the beach, but rather at water's edge. There's a certain kind of—I think I've noticed—footwork, it seems, very much to pattern. We sort of talked and I found out, in fact, that she was hardly from some exotic site abroad, but rather, a gal from Georgia who was down there with her daughter, who also was named Phoebe.

MB: The Dirty Phoebes.

GL: Yes, the Dirty Phoebes. It was amazing. It was the kind of experience one could have when one's mother was lying dying. That was the notion of the novel I had, that I would have this projection of myself, to be present at the deathwatch and then, as I'm sure many writers before me have written, find a way to elude for a moment, to escape for a moment, to go off and have some phantasm occur, and feel guilty about it, thereafter. (pause) And I sort of did. I did this time with my mother. I saw Phoebe that night, Dirty Phoebe that night, on the beach again, on the beach again, yes. You say, do I love the women I'm with? Well, let me tell you. When I was standing there at water's edge, with Dirty Phoebe, there wasn't one spicule of the phenomenon that constitutes Dirty Phoebe, for me, of that human being, for me, that I was not supremely conscious of. That, I call a kind of love. I mean, I can this moment recollect with the greatest of ease all of those phenomena that might make, in some sense, at least superficially, the person, Dirty Phoebe—what the pores in her skin were doing in this region of her arm as against that region of her arm as against that region of her arm, in reaction to the cold water, and so on.

MB: One hundred-percent concentration.

GL: Yes, yes, a form of attention, which I think we are agreed, is what art is all about. It's also what lovemaking is all about, a form of attention.

MB: You said once that you had never been in love. Would you say that again?
GL: Well, that's a very tricky question for me to answer.

MB: Well, you can try.
GL: If one were to adopt the same kind of logical turn of mind that animates yours, in so far as you are able to declare it, then one would demand a definition of the term, and so on.

MB: You can define it yourself.
GL: I could define "never," too.

MB: Sure.
GL: And keep on with definitions until we got absolutely nowhere.

MB: Not sure I agree with that, but you could try to define it, or redefine it.
GL: I think that I have had such a feeling. I certainly have such a feeling in the course of . . . but would this be sustainable outside of that context? My answer would be, in so far as I can see, well, sort of, yes. That sounds like a very unemphatic verdict.

MB: Or not answering the question.
GL: Not a very vigorous way to reply.

MB: Ambiguous.
GL: But certainly the unambiguous thing to say is this is ambiguous; or rather, to say that this is ambiguous would prove to be very unambiguous in relation to telling one's truth.

MB: Then maybe you could say you've never been in love or you've loved and do love all the women.
GL: Yes, it would mean the same thing then. But would meaning matter? What has meaning got to do with it? What matters is time, not meaning.

MB: Oh, I think meaning matters.
GL: I think time matters, getting more of it, extending it. My most recent formulation: I would say that, in a reductive way, it's all intensity and extensity, just intensity and extensity. If you could take this in the acoustical relation to words, maybe it would be propensity. You're looking for meaning;

that would be propensity. You know what I'm getting at? I'm looking for another word. So I can say it's my intensity and extensity against your intentionality. But meaning? I just don't see the property of meaning at all. It just seems to me to be a fool's game, obviously, fraught with naught but error.

MB: Santayana said: "To understand oneself is the classic form of consolation."
GL: Yes, you read that to me.

MB: "And to elude oneself is the romantic."
GL: He must have been citing Socrates in the first instance.

MB: But what I'm asking you is do you think you might be the romantic? Maybe you don't want meaning? Is that what you mean?
GL: Now I think you're ganging up on me with your knowledge. Hang on, I'm not too sure that there isn't some kind of trouble with our nouns here. You say, in the first instance, that I don't want meaning—

MB: Or knowledge. Let's say knowledge.
GL: Or knowing, because it might, in some way, displace the program of not knowing with feeling, in the sense of living in one's senses, and that the two are somehow in opposition; that you can't hold these ways of being in concinnity, and have the virtues of both. Do I think that?

MB: I don't know. I don't think that.
GL: I think if you take time as your boundary in this case—I thought we were talking in absolutes—that we're not looking for any kind of qualifications here. But I do think that since life is the only Good, more life is better. If you can try to make more life for yourself by exploiting the units of time given you in greater detail with something approaching an absolute form of attention, then I think you are doing the best you can to get the best deal you can with the lousy rap that you've got coming to you. So I don't know what meaning has to do with any of this. Well, okay, by living in pursuit of meaning, I achieve precisely those two values—intensity and extensity. By proposing that meaning matters, entirely, I'm giving myself a greater sense of intensity. So I'm achieving the same battle risings of behavior that you have. We just speak a different code. We have different substitutions.

MB: I'd agree.
GL: I didn't answer your question terribly well at all.

MB: I think it's a difficult question and I didn't pose it as well as I could have. So we can come back to it another time. But with respect to the way that you think, and in listening to you speak—
GL: Why don't you simplify that for me and give me one subject.

MB: All right.
GL: Who's the agency in this, you or me?

MB: You. Let me ask you a question.
GL: Go on. You start.

MB: Who do you think has had the greatest influence on your thinking—and parents are a given this time, so you must leave them out.
GL: Well, my Aunt Adele probably, the younger sister of my mother, whom I took to be the most attractive person around. I liked the way she was, the way she looked, the way she bore herself about, the way she seemed to think about herself. I copied her a lot.

MB: What about in the nut house?
GL: What?

MB: The loony bin.
GL: The loony bin was Hayden Carruth, a man I had the very good fortune to come across, an inmate who had had a very colorful career—not colorful, but distinguished career—as a young man in the literary magazine world, and who also was recognized as a hot young comer—as a poet, namely, Hayden Carruth. He had an enormous impact on me. I guess because I was sixteen. I think I was. I don't know how old he was. He turned eighty-one just recently and I turned sixty-eight. I'll let you do the arithmetic. I just admired the hell out of him. I began to admire him, first, I think, because he smoked a pipe. I thought that was really a noble-looking thing to do, and the pipe was the right shape and he smoked it right and he didn't make a big thing of it. He was reading the *Partisan Review* one day, and I had an exchange with him. I used the word "idea." He said: "Idea, idea, you don't even know what an idea is. Why don't you

take this magazine, this journal here, and read it and maybe you'll see an idea on exhibition." I think he was the first person in my life ever to say anything of such rank. I mean, I was being talked to in a kind of serious way, even though it was as one would talk to a child, but it was serious. He, in that sense, began to take me under his wing. I became very, very fond of Hayden—and saw him not too long ago at a function given here in New York, in his honor, when he turned eighty-one years old—though I never thought very much of Hayden as a poet. Even then, I thought of him as somebody who knew that poetry was serious, knew that there was a special kind of circumstance that whatever seriousness one might have that was not of that kind would be inferior to it. It was the only way to be in the world. I learned something from Hayden: That the only superpower is language. The only superpower is grammar.

MB: Then he had a great influence, second to Aunt Adele?
GL: Oh, yes, even though I knew that he was not really a very good poet. I was a kid, but I could tell that.

MB: But in terms of the direction of your life, the life you'd make after that?
GL: Yes, sure, sure, but now my great sense in delight in poetry would be because of Jack Gilbert, not Hayden Carruth.

MB: As a poet.
GL: And as an influence. It's indisputable that much of Gilbert's way of hearing, I seem to have taken on for myself, his way of hearing a line.

MB: How long have you known Gilbert?
GL: We met, I think it was—I came to New York in 1969—so it was about 1960.

MB: Out in California.
GL: Maybe '59, '60, yes, in California, San Francisco. He was recently returned from Perugia, Italy, where he had spent some many years, and nothing could have been as exotic as this. Just the words "Perugia, Italy," that was for me as exciting as you could get. He'd been there, and he had returned from there, and he was a fellow with a name that was alongside the names of the poets that you mainly were hearing at a two-week reading being sponsored by the museum of modern art there—names like Brother Antoninus, Sister Mary Gilbert, Lawrence Ferlinghetti, Allen Ginsberg. They

had a lot more theater in them. And this was a rather flat Welsh name, Jack Gilbert. He presented himself not in the usual kind of theatrical garb, but just a navy blue suit and a white shirt and a red tie. He struck quite a figure. And then he began intoning—in the most earnest way—love songs, poetry. Magnificent, I couldn't really get enough of it. I went up to him at the close of his reading and embraced him, picked him up off the floor and embraced him, and said: "Come on back to Burlingame with my wife and me. He needed a meal. He was undernourished and he was happy to eat. Jack never changed. He was always happy to eat. He looked as if he got by on simply pebbles, never had any money, never would concede to doing a job. He had some grants, that sort of thing, to help him out, and I think he taught a term or two at Smith College.

MB: So what about Kesey and Cassady and those fellows? What kind of influence did they have on you?

GL: None at all, none at all, none at all. No, by that time I was long past being influenced, if you're meaning with respect to my own writing. No, no, no, only writing, only the way I might hear a sentence, or the way in which syntax would present itself as something to think about. That was all formed long before I met Kesey and Cassady. Kesey and Cassady were rather more instructive on how to live than how to write. Between the two, I certainly felt that Cassady was the more expert. Kesey—I didn't much approve of the way he lived. I suppose because I was rather judgmental about his treatment of his children. Cassady was free of this charge because Cassady was childless. No, wait, Cassady had children. He had three children and he abandoned them. Oh, my gosh, I forgot. That's right. He had John, and those two girls. He abandoned his children, really abandoned them. So I guess Kesey did the better job. Shame, shame, shame, shame. Wow. I admired the hell out of both of those guys. And I really loved Cassady. He was a lovable man.

MB: This was back in your Arizona days?

GL: No, no, this was still California, San Francisco. Although Kesey came out to see me once when I was separated from my first wife and I was living in Dallas. Kesey came out to see me, I think to read out there, something like that. So I saw him there and we had a high old time for a couple of days. But, yes, Kesey was the most charismatic. With Kesey, you just promptly fell in the thrall. He just overtook you in no time. The same way Cassady would overtake you. But, you know, Kesey really had charisma. Cassady did not. Cassady had vitality.

MB: Looks.

GL: Vitality, and looks, and godliness, if there is such a thing. He was an angelically dear man. But Kesey had a quality that really could bring to him, did bring to him, in my opinion, scores of acolytes who would camp around, in hope of deriving from his presence, some kind of benison for themselves. I was one. I was one of Kesey's acolytes. I felt blessed in his company. There was a benevolence that issued from him, something that came from a supernatural force. There was that. This existed around Kesey. And I know I resented it a lot when I first was buddies with him, because there was a clutch of kids around him all the time, diverting his attention from himself and trivializing his life. That style of living seemed to persist from that day forward. After *Cuckoo's Nest* was out, he became a figure of a certain cultish interest. He really had something quite apart from his writing and everything else. He had a way of being with people. It was mesmerizing, really mesmerizing. You felt the countenance of something lifted up and shone upon you in Kesey's presence.

MB: Remarkable.

GL: And you liked having his approval, I guess, but you felt it was never really quite granted. I'm interested in hearing myself saying these things about Kesey because they're really true. The other day I was with one of my kids having breakfast, and I said Kesey's name, and I was so startled when I said it because I was immediately unable to remember that he had died just barely a month ago. It was strange to see the name of someone of such corpulence, in your memory, who is now gone. He was such a force.

MB: Which of your books do you like the best?

GL: Oh, you know, I can do that with my children, but I can't do that with my books, probably because the affection for my books is greater than that for my children.

MB: (laughter) Recently.

GL: You mean the best in the sense of which I would look at? I might read the beginning of *Zimzum*. More than anything else, I might do that. I think it has the fewest errors in it. I can see the errors in it. There are about eight or nine, in that first crot, but I've learned to live with the errors. Usually, when I pick up something that's been printed, the error rate becomes so great for me, I am too distracted to read and I become upset. I want to rewrite this and rewrite that. But in that opening crot in *Zimzum*, I seem to find the fewest to be upset about.

MB: You said once you didn't read *Epigraph* after it was in print.
GL: No, I still haven't read it, no, but then I haven't read any of them all the way through. I might have ultimately read a story collection, maybe a story one day, another story another day, but no novel.

MB: Why not *Epigraph?* You don't like it?
GL: No, I read the first few letters. I read up until it started to get a little funny for me.

MB: Funny, meaning?
GL: Well, I mean there's a line where I say: "Can I see your tits?" or something like that. He's writing to one of the nurses. (laughter) I can't read it when I get to that part. (laughs) I become tickled.

MB: So you start laughing at yourself? Oh, I see. You really meant funny.
GL: Yes, yes, yes. (laughter) "Let me see your tits." (laughter) He's trying to entice one of the nurses back to his house for tea. (laughter) And he realizes she may be married. So he says: "I'll be right back. I didn't mean anything by it." (laughter)

MB: (laughter) Well, this leads right into the question of your reputation. Some would say you've got quite a reputation.
GL: I'm so glad. Certainly the actuality could not rival the fiction. Nevertheless, we must understand, that the fiction has its magnitude only because the actuality has a corresponding magnitude.

MB: Yes.
(pause)
GL: Life has been good. Life is good.

MB: Yes.
GL: Life is good and God is great. (laughter)

MB: Have you got something to eat?
GL: I've got matzo.

MB: And butter?
GL: No butter, but I've got some yellow grease in a tub.

Interview with Gordon Lish

John Lee and Vernon Chatman / 2009

From *The Believer*, 59, January 2009, pp. 71–76. © 2009 John Lee and Vernon Chatman. Reprinted by permission.

Lish's list on writing:
1. Loosened association
2. Antic behavior
3. Autism
4. Morbid ambivalence

Ignore the fact that he's written about eating shit, or about stabbing someone in the eye and hearing the particular click as the knife tip punctures a contact lens. Forget the fact that he was so sure Dean Moriarty was a real person that he moved his entire family to San Francisco to hang out with "the man," or that he published a story under the pretext that it was written by Salinger. Gordon Lish is the Andy Kaufman of the literary world. A maniac of publishing, wit, dessert, Mr. Lish is a mythic figure—a supra-monster, distorting and bending American fiction in its own shiny be-stabbed eye.

At the peak of his powers, Lish dubbed himself "Captain Fiction." As a teacher (for Gary Lutz, Amy Hempel, Will Eno, etc.) he railed for perfect, compressed sentences; as an editor (for Raymond Carver, *Esquire*, *The Quarterly*, etc.) he slashed and compacted with line-item-veto fury; and as a novelist (the infuriatingly riveting *Extravaganza*: *A Joke Book*) he is capable of some of the most grandiose, gleeful overindulgences imaginable. He has long ceased publishing and writing, but his influence is out there, watching you, breathing.

Lish and friends used to meet and eat weekly in the now-defunct "Pork Store" on Broadway and Broome—Lish's favorite haven for marinated meats—where he would hold court with whoever was within arm's reach. Because he is so reluctant to answer any question put directly into his face,

and since most of his novels are written in letter-form, we were forced/ honored to interview him via chicken-scratch postcards. The results are a hodge-podge ball of randomalia that leak secret truths about a "man" who is unknowable, untouchable, un-unintelligible.
—John Lee and Vernon Chatman

Dear Mr. Lish,
1. Can you infuriate people into liking you?
2. Does it matter? The infuriation. The liking.
3. What is that which hammered you into the shape you are in?
4. What matters most? (A list.)
5. Describe the perfect description.

John Lee

Gordon Lish replies:
According to my staff, this was to have been a one-question, per leg, letteration. Yet you ask, in yours last, excuse me, five questions. Tell you what: I'll, to the best of my ability, answer *one*, a word I just had to italicize at my own expense, and another, if we are counting all such exertions obtained from me so far—replying to one of the five, you see—em dashes, earlier, ignored at the worsening peril. To wit: what is that which hammered you into the shape you are in? All right, if this is what you want to know. I, Gordon Lish, will tell you what hammered me into the shape I am in. Was maybe seven, when, come summer, was required to spend it killing Japanese beetles. Oh, and, remaining bent to the grass, dig out, tear out, wrench out—with all my defeated wiles—crabgrass.

Yours truly, etc.
Gordon Lish

Dear Gordon Lish,
Vernon and I saw you read at the Fez almost a decade ago. You started to read a story, but then interrupted yourself to look at your watch, and got confused because it wasn't on your wrist. While looking for your watch in all your pockets, you proceeded to tell an entire story about your father. Then you got a little overheated and felt sick. We always thought this entire thing was an act and we loved it, but it wasn't. You were actually getting sick. You were actually in need of help. How can we take you seriously when we don't know the difference between the truth and the act?

John Lee

Gordon Lish replies:
There is no realm wherein we have the truth. All endeavor is an act, including, of course, the composing of this postcard. Oh, there is one exception, City Bakery's peanut butter cookies. On the other hand, a baker baking is an act.

Dear Gordon Lish,
Last night I had a dream. You, Vernon, Alyson, some tour guide/private detective, and myself were swimming in a bay just north of Hollywood. The private eye was not the most informed guide, but we forgave him because we concluded PIs are about gathering information and not teaching. I decided to swim ashore, only to come across a beach covered with thousands of half-birthed sea turtle eggs. Not wanting to crush them, I tried to wade through the shallow water, but that ended up bruising the eggs. My dilemma was to crush a few or bruise many.

I woke up and wondered why you were in the dream, and two thoughts came to mind. I could have waded in the water, waited for the eggs to hatch, hurting none of the turtles. And, you, Gordon Lish, are about accuracy and jokes, not about interpretations and dreams. So, my question for you is this: what's the funniest dream you've ever had?
John Lee

Dear Questioner,
You are asking me, Gordon Lish, what is my funniest dream? So since when is there such a thing in the world as a funny dream? I am telling you, in all of my life I, Gordon Lish, have yet to undergo the experience of what a person, in this person's right mind, could intelligently refer to as a funny dream. Let me give you every assurance that not once in all of my days—not nights?— have I, Gordon Lish, even possibly chuckled a little bit when, you know, when officially asleep.
Yours in truth,
Gordon Lish

Mr. Lish,
Mr. Lish, Mr. Lish. Only you can answer these questions directed only at you and for your eyes only, Mr Lish. I come to you with desperation tearing at the throat of my fingers as they strike the keys of my board, Mr. Lish. My keyboard, Mr. Lish, for the typing. But with each individual word (oh shit, maybe could it be with each individual letter?) that passes under your cruel

gaze, you grow ever more disappointed, I fear. Ever more bored with every wasteful key I press, each extraneous button I push, I will skip right along to the point forthwith and posthaste. In kissing adieu to all further ado, I steal now away through the dark night of these preliminaries to illuminate for you the (main) matter at (freshly washed, I can assure you) hand.

You see, I had a terrible dream last night, which left its claws in my gash of a mind of a brain, that is to say, only you can soothe it. You, if you haven't yet been moistened to death. In a tub of Jergens, yet.

My dream remains fuzzy, so I fight all of speed and time to get it all down: I dreamed, I fear, that my friend and your associate John Lee had a dream about you. His dream, thankfully, remains woefully clear in the frozen bank of my memory's chamber.

In his dream (that I had) you were you—but you were also an institution. Do you know, a building? Made of stone and concrete. A structure itself, on the Upper East Side of Manhattan. And folks, specifically folks who knew what they were after, would pile inside and get what their hearts told them to take away and then file right on out again. This continued until boulders began tumbling out of your uppermost windows. They were large and rough and they damaged other buildings as they rolled, but left not a scratch on any man. And from every (eventually) halted boulder there grew, eventually, a harem. These ladies were plenty good enough and plenty game enough to fill the rest of the night for me. But soon they fell apart where they stood, and lay, disemboweled as though from your imagination, Mr. Lish.

Oh, I know you are not interested in dreams.

Kindly send me your thoughts on this issue, or kindly cruelly reject the idea of sending me your thoughts on this matter forthwith, and please, do, if you can (and can you must), answer in good form of an institution. For reference.
Vernon

Gordon Lish replies:
See a doctor. Have you seen a doctor? My advice is for you to see a Jewish doctor. See a Jewish mental doctor.
Love and kisses,
Also, eat at Frank's.

Dear Mr. Lish,
I greedily inhaled your letter pockmarked July 14, advising me to seek the services of a Jewish mental doctor. Vilst my Jew doc savior remains unsook,

what a wonderful opportunity for you to tell me about the nuthouse. Did it help for you to be in the nuthouse? Was there value in it? What if anything did you get out of your nuthousular experience?
Vernon Chatman

Gordon Lish replies:
Terrific. It imparted to me the appearance of a quality not to be had by other means.

Dear Mr. Lish,
When you were in the bobby hatch, did you write? Did you get to touch any of the boobies?
Vernon Chatman

Gordon Lish replies:
Yes, yes, to "touch" them over the eight-month course of my opportunity to "touch" some of them—two whilst (one could mingle with the be-boobied ladies for an hour a week when one had attained a residence on an open ward), and then another two of these thereafterward. My stars, just how crazy do you fellows think I was!

Dear Gordon Lish,
Why "Captain Fiction"? What are your powers?
John Lee

Gordon Lish replies:
Captain Fiction's powers? There are seven of them. One is the power to see the heart of the writer through a single word. The other six I forgot.
Yours in Christ,
G.L.

Dear Mr. Lish,
In the mental place, what did the mental doctors say about you?
Vernon Chatman

Gordon Lish replies:
What did "the mental doctors say about me in the mental place"? Well, sir or Sir, they did not say it to me, save for one psychiatrist. He came to chat with me the day of my being discharged, advising that I not stay at the dog fight until the last dog was dead. I was a kid and made little of this counsel.

Now that I am a bigger kid, I see the value—belatedly—added. Yet I also see the loss of life in the protecting, first of all, of oneself. Better to give oneself away. Dead fuck the dog and so on.

Dear Mr. Lish,
The other day in the Pork Store, as I was savaging a plate of pork with my jagged mouth, you said that you are both repelled by and attracted to the sight of violence. I once saw a man getting his head slammed against a curb while the gathered chanted "Burrito! Burrito!" (the assailant's nom de guerre) as they were, really, splashed with blood. And you said that one way to escape being haunted by visions of this kind of violence was to write about them. How does that work? And how much of your writing do you think is exorcism?
Vernon Chatman

Gordon Lish replies:
No, I am not "haunted" by "visions" of violence. What I said was this: if violence comes within my (ken?), I am both repelled and compelled by it, terrified yet delighted, fastened to the sight of it, yet aching to run away, at least to turn away, but that I find that I succumb to the desire to look, am transfixed, am spellbound, am made mad, appalled but enthralled. All writing rids the writer of his accomplices, these being the events of his life insofar as he can recall them and deform them for purposes of personal disguise.
P.S. This is a borrowed ballpoint.

Dear Gordon Lish,
When people ask about what made us, we tell them—read Lish, watch Buñuel, and listen to ODB. What do you tell people? What made you?
John Lee

Gordon Lish replies:
Quim.
(a.k.a. ginch, gash, gumbo.)

Dear Mr. Lish,
When they talk about you, what do you like them to say about you?
Vernon Chatman

Gordon Lish replies:
That he was a man who knew the value of a cookie. Also the ditto of nookie.

Dear Mr. Lish,
The other day, in the Pork Store, you indicated, in your way, that it's important for one to have enemies the way some people (like, for example, you) collect wives. Why is it good or important to have enemies? Who is on the shit Lisht?
Vernon Chatman

Gordon Lish replies:
My father's first, even though he was perfectly swell to me and did all he could do to supply me with safety and probably loved me as much as a father must. Yet, yeah, he was the first person I made an enemy out of and was tickled pink about it.

Dear Gordon,
You mentioned that you moved to San Francisco hoping to meet Dean Moriarty. And that after reading Salinger, you truly believed that the Glass family was real. Do you consider this the unique gift of fiction—to immerse you so much in characters as to inspire the delusion that they are real?
Yours,
Vernon Chatman

Gordon Lish replies:
So, how were the eats at Frank's?

Dear Gordon Lish,
Doesn't the contract, the fantasy, if you will, fall on the shoulders of the bookworm? Shouldn't the reader pour his heart and soul into a book, committing every word to truth?
John Lee

Gordon Lish replies:
That's right. Committed. It was an involuntary committal. I was absolutely eligible.

Mr. Lish,
The other day at the Pork Store, you failed to bring up the fact that your "novel in jokes," *Extravaganza,* is "literally" a paradox, in that it is "literature" which concerns itself with a "pair" of "docs" (or doctors, if you will), the primary paradox being that only one of them is actually a doctor (or

"doc," if you will) and the secondary (or self-canceling) paradox being that the book is not, in fact, actually, it turns out, a paradox at all. My question for you is: Do you who create and craft literature ever find literary analysis tedious? Pointless? Or lame? (Circle one and explain.)
Vernon Chatman

Gordon Lish replies:
Listen, buster, I, Gordon, am not circling anything, OK?

Mr. Lish,
Of course I know that "Lish Is Love," but illuminate for me one more time, articulate for me why is Lish love?
Vernon Chatman

Gordon Lish replies:
Why is Lish, you ask, in love? Lish is in love by reason of all that has given all others to claim themselves in love. Except in Lish's case, it's rather more special on account of its being Lish's case.

Dear Mr. Lish,
I thank you kindly for answering the question "Why is Lish in love." But the question I really wanted answered is "Why is Lish love?" Meaning, why does Mr. Gordon Lish embody Love itself? Why is it that you are a living embodiment of Love itself?
Vernon Chatman

Gordon Lish replies:
As a stratagem, I say—to evade invasion, I say. To keep all comers at bay, I say. Intactness first. The proproprium is prime, all be it pussy is really nice too—once you're, you know, as Seneca says, cured.

Dear Gordon Lish,
Below is a list that I posted over my bed that you, Gordon Lish, created about writing. Can you tell me a story that explains this list?
   1. Loosened association.
   2. Antic behavior.
   3. Autism.
   4. Morbid ambivalence.
John Lee

Gordon Lish replies:
The items listed concern the devising of a method I once advocated as productive of a state conducive to the creation of an act of imaginative writing different from all other acts of the kind, the aim being to bring about an artifact of singular character. There might have been a fifth cue also possessed of an initial A. But there just as well might not have been. How many components would you say contrive to effect the singularity of a City Bakery peanut-butter cookie?

Dear Gordon Lish,
Cookies are on the way. Shall drop some off with your doorman sometime soon. Get your mouth ready.

Gordon Lish replies:
Thanks.

Dear Gordon,
In all your years of teaching, who was your favorite student? And which child of yours is your favorite child?
Vernon Chatman

Gordon Lish replies:
In all the hours of my teaching, I, Gordon, by far, was my favorite student. Same goes for my favorite child—it was never not I. But if there were a peanut-butter cookie in it for me, I'd say whatever you said I should.

[*The cookies are delivered.*]

Gordon Lish replies:
Never in all my days have I been as tested. Get this: Beloved is making for to depart. There is discovered on the monopodium at the door a paper bag, a note. Beloved says, "What's this?" inspecting. Gordo guesses, then in folly says, "Oh, it must be the peanut-butter cookies promised me by Chatman and Lee." The lady tarries, eatingly. Or eatishly?

Dear Gordon Lish,
You've talked about being the ghost author of many titles—I won't reveal names because you've asked me not to—but did you, Gordon Lish, write a book called *Mysterium*? It's on the Internet as your having written such a book. Should I correct this, or do you take credit for it?
John Lee

Gordon Lish replies:
I wrote a book and called it *Mysterium*. It was to have been my last novel. I withdrew the thing from publication when I had read to page forty-five of the first proofs. How there occurs any reference to any of this anywhere beats, scares, the piss out of me. Are you fellows setting yourselves up to get to be brand-new enemies of mine?

Dear Gordon Lish,
I've read accounts of your teachings and classes. A lot of people didn't like the process. They felt abused, berated, and destroyed. Yet, in the end of it all, they felt like you did teach them something. So my question to you, Gordon Lish, is this: can you infuriate people into liking you?
Vernon Chatman

Gordon Lish replies:
Three people appear to "like" me. Two of them appear to be "you and Vernon." The third person begs to keep herself unidentified. None appears to have been bullied into "liking" me, but people—hah, "people"!—and their much-vaunted appearances, are you serious?

Dear Lish,
Who has been your greatest teacher?
Vernon Chatman

Gordon Lish replies:
In the classroom? Oliver Sigworth—for the style of his pacing—preening—posing, or is it posturing? Reminiscent of the Matador Manolete. Not in a classroom? Emmanuel Levinas.

Dear Gordon Lish,
You, Gordon Lish, have written a few novels. Some of those communicated through letters. What is it about the letter that you like?
John Lee

Gordon Lish replies:
The literacy of it.

Dear Mr. Lish,
You, as you know, are a man who, as you are aware, likes to have his lid flipped—what, then, was the last, the most recent piece of artistical expression

(this sentence notwithstanding) that truly flipped (true psychosis excepted) your infamous lid?
Vernon Chatman

Gordon Lish replies:
Most recent instantiation? McCarthy's *The Road*. Read it a couple of weeks ago and it still has me by the neck. Also DeLillo's new play *Love-Lies-Bleeding*. Lidishly speaking.

Dear Gordon Lish,
Who edited your books?
John Lee

Gordon Lish replies:
You're conning me, right? But what I could use an editor for is for keeping me from using the same preposition more than once when I answer somebody's question. Or is it, like, you know, an adverb?

Gordon Lish, The Art of Editing No. 2

Christian Lorentzen / 2015

From *The Paris Review*, Winter 2015, pp. 195–216. Reprinted by permission.

It's the custom for editors to keep a low profile and to underplay any changes they may make to an author's manuscript. Gordon Lish is a different animal. Not since Maxwell Perkins has an editor been so famous—or notorious—as a sculptor of other people's prose. As fiction editor of *Esquire* from 1969 to 1977, then as an editor at Knopf and of *The Quarterly* until 1995, Lish worked closely with many of the most daring writers of the past fifty years, including Harold Brodkey, Raymond Carver, Don DeLillo, Barry Hannah, and Joy Williams. In an interview with this magazine in 2004, Hannah said, "Gordon Lish was a genius editor. A deep friend and mentor. He taught me how to write short stories. He would cross out everything so there'd be like three lines left, and he would be right."

His collaborations have not always ended amicably. His editorial relationship with Carver ceased after three books. When Lish donated his papers to the Lilly Library at Indiana University Bloomington, they indeed showed that he had drastically cut, and often rewritten, some of Carver's best loved stories. For the *Collected Stories*, published in 2009, Carver's widow printed some of them in both edited and unedited versions. The critical reaction was divided. In the *New York Times Book Review*, Stephen King described the effect on one story as "a total rewrite ... a cheat"; in *The New York Review of Books*, Giles Harvey wrote that the publication of Carver's unedited stories "has not done Carver any favors. Rather, it has inadvertently pointed up the editorial genius of Gordon Lish."

More than a dozen books have appeared under Lish's own name—including the novels *Dear Mr. Capote* (1983), *Peru* (1986), and *Zimzum* (1993). These have won Lish a small but passionate cult following as a writer of recursive and often very funny prose. For decades he taught legendary classes in fiction, both at institutions such as Yale and Columbia and in private sessions in New York and across America. Though he titled one of his books *Arcade, or, How to Write a Novel* (1999), he, like Socrates, never put his teachings on paper. They survive in his students, many of whom are now prominent writers and teachers of fiction, among them Christine Schutt, Sam Lipsyte, Gary Lutz, and Ben Marcus.

Lish was born in 1934 in Hewlett, New York, the son of a hat manufacturer and a housewife. In early childhood he was afflicted with acute psoriasis, a condition that has persisted all his life. After being kicked out of Andover, he spent the rest of his teens and twenties working in radio and at odd jobs in New York; Pampa, Texas; and Tucson, where he eventually received a B.A. from the University of Arizona. Even now he has retained the smooth baritone and cultured vowels of a 1950s disc jockey. After his first marriage, to Frances Fokes, ended in divorce, he married Barbara Works; he lives in the Upper East Side apartment that he shared with his second wife until her death from ALS in 1994. The interview was conducted in his living room, over several long sessions that began in the spring of 2010 and ended last September. Often we would be interrupted by phone calls from Lish's friends and former students, some of them seeking advice on the finishing stages of their books. He was a convivial host, offering his interviewer bottles of beer and a large brass pot for use as an ashtray.

Christian Lorentzen: Do you consider yourself a writer or an editor?
Gordon Lish: I'm not a writer. I've no stake in my being thought a writer. Yet if I do write, I want it to be as exacting as I can make it. I want whatever I doodle to be well doodled. Most of the writing I've done has been under other names, as a ghostwriter, to maintain my family. Or else by writing potboilers. Not that such endeavors could necessarily be told apart.

Q: For example?
A: The only one I admit to is called *Coming Out of the Ice,* which Harcourt, I think it was, published in 1979. It concerns Victor Herman, who, in his teens, was taken to Russia by his communist family—this in the thirties. After a while, the mother and children wanted to come back to the States. Victor's father had collected his family's passports and Victor and his siblings were stuck in Russia. He went on to achieve fame as the Lindbergh of Russia by his having parachuted from an airplane at a record height—an altitude greater than theretofore had been jumped from—and come down

chewing on an apple, a rather sporty feat that caught the attention of the American press. He thereafter spent seventeen years in the gulags. Herman was repatriated during Ford's term, Kissinger having intervened. Harcourt had a contract with him for his story, and I was called in and I checked with Bill Buckley, asking who could tell me if the guy was kosher. Buckley phoned so-and-so, and she said, "Doesn't look right to me." I agreed to do the work anyway, desperate to make the fee. It was sixty thousand dollars. I went out to Detroit to interview Victor maybe six weekends. Herman was a man in his sixties, and he seemed to relish the bitter cold while he was dressed in a short-sleeved shirt. It was as though his having lived in Siberia, seventy-five degrees below zero, had conditioned him for such weather. I can sit from seven in the morning to seven at night without urinating. Victor seemed eager to prove he could do the same. We sat in a motel room, Victor declining a break. That was also impressive. In the end, I had to make up a lot of the book because Victor's account was, to my mind, preposterous. I made up a character I called Red, a Finn, who proved critical in seeing to Victor's survival, teaching him, for example, how, for food, to trap rats in the latrine. About three years after I finished the book—Victor didn't live long after this—Victor phoned me to say, "You're not gonna believe it, you're not gonna believe it! Red has turned up!"

Q: Before you were a ghostwriter or an editor, you were in radio.
A: I auditioned to be an announcer at NBC when I was about sixteen. I was given an audition by Pat Kelly, then chief of announcers. He went along with me in great kindness. My aim was ridiculous. I had been thrown out of Andover.

Q: How did you get kicked out of Andover?
A: Fighting, fighting. Some fellow, or fellows, called me a dirty Jew, and I was a fighter. A small, a little, fighter. Kelly said, "We don't take people who haven't been to college." I said, "I'm not going to college." He said, "Well, go out to the lobby and look in the back of *Broadcasting Magazine* for a want ad and find someplace as far from New York as you can." I saw an ad for Pampa, Texas, and thought, "That's around where California is, so isn't that far away enough?" I went to my father's office and after a couple of phone calls, I was hired that day and flew out to Pampa, after having first gone to J. Press to dress myself accordingly, figuring I was quite the fellow now. Nothing could have been sillier.

Q: So you got the job?

A: I did. And stayed and stayed, and then, owing to my skin, had to come back to New York. It was then that I was put on ACTH for pretty terrible psoriasis. ACTH prefigured cortisone, so far as I know, and hydrocortisone. It saved my bacon. A couple of injections and I was on the way to what I had never before seen—clear skin. I also ended up in the bughouse in White Plains, possibly as the result of the steroid therapy. Something similar became the subject of a *New Yorker* article and a movie called *Bigger Than Life.* James Mason was in it as a schoolteacher given cortisone for some disorder and who then winds up quite wacked out. But then, as I aged, I think I preferred thinking I had been authentically psychotic and that the ACTH was merely coincidental. I suppose I wanted to be as crazy as the next one. Maybe crazier. After eight months in the mental place, I was given ACTH again. It was then that I got jobs on radio in New Haven and here in New York. I was a disc jockey, first at a restaurant called Johnny Johnston's Charcoal Room on Forty-Fifth and Second—this in the fifties. Thereafter, I was moved to the studio out in Livingston, New Jersey, and broadcast from twelve till two in the morning, trying to mimic Jean Shepherd, who was, by my lights, the most interesting person on radio. He would improvise thoroughly charming tales. I found his work riveting, simply riveting. Then he went into television and that didn't pan out for him, couldn't quite effect the magic he enacted so ingeniously on radio. I tried to copy Shepherd's manner, but failed utterly. Passed out one night—it turned out by reason of my having developed hypokalemia owing to the ACTH. So then I was taken out to Tucson as an invalid. Was told I had to live there for the sun and aridity. I was nineteen and I was informed I had to remain in Tucson and keep myself out of doors as much as could be managed. I worked as a wrangler at a dude ranch for a while, and then sought a job in radio. A woman I'd seen on local TV interviewed me, and I was hired to do wake-up radio for the NBC affiliate. I married the woman but never showed up for the job. That's Frances—Frances Fokes. She had done very well at Wellesley. That was our form of contact. My father had wanted my sister to attend Wellesley, but she did not, and he was heartbroken by this. So here it was, a kind of supplemental gesture on my part—I'll furnish you a daughter-in-law who's gone to Wellesley. The marriage lasted eight or nine years and produced three children, Jennifer, Rebecca, and Ethan. We lived on chicken backs and beans. Frances had a program of her own, an interview show around noon, and she was also a salesperson at the station. But I, having notions that married women should properly be supported, encouraged her to quit and for us to rely on what I could make as a door-to-door health-insurance salesman—this, it later became clear, for what was not an entirely legitimate outfit.

Q: Were you successful?
A: I was, until I panicked and sent a certified letter to the company indicating that I had become aware of practices that were not in keeping with propriety and that I was resigning. I was scared to death I would be sent to jail. I was being driven around by two guys in a pink, radically tail-finned Plymouth. We would raid the impoverished neighborhoods on the outskirts of Tucson, signing up anybody in sight and pocketing all of the first premium—premiums which had to be paid in cash. We'd save a dollar to send to the company and keep the rest. There was, I suppose, no evidence of there being any company.

Q: Did it ever make it back to you when these people made claims?
A: I was long gone in no time at all. I got out of there and got on the road. I had been smitten with Kerouac, as I had been with Salinger, and had taken it all in without any sense that this indeed was fiction. I ate it up, and wanted to place myself among, or between, Dean Moriarty and Sal Paradise. Truly.

Q: So you went to California and found Neal Cassady?
A: I became good buddies with Cassady for about four years. Never met Kerouac. At one point, Cassady had batches of letters from John Clellon Holmes and William S. Burroughs and Ginsberg and Kerouac that he wanted to sell. One was a lot of twelve and another a lot of thirteen. I sold them for a total of twenty-five hundred dollars to Andreas Brown, the fellow who ended up owning Frances Steloff's Gotham Book Mart.

Cassady was always trying to get some money together for a gift for Carolyn, for an anniversary, say. They were married twice—therefore, two anniversaries. Ran into Neal for the last time. Barbara and I were traveling in Mexico. My second wife and I, that is. I was in search of a psoriasis cure rumored to be had in Chihuahua and had money from *A Man's Work*, a series of interview recordings I'd done for McGraw-Hill. We were seated in probably the one place in town on the main drag where people would gather to have a Coke, and Cassady came rolling along with George Walker, who was one of the Kesey retinue, one of the crew on the bus. Barbara liked Cassady, which seemed to me highly unlikely, because Barbara absolutely did not approve of Kesey. I had severed relations with all of that number while I was going through the divorce from Frances, thinking that it had gotten me in trouble when teaching and it would certainly do ditto when the case came to court. Barbara and I went off with Cassady to some party, and at about four in the morning, I can recall Neal and I were standing around in a driveway, and Cassady was asking, "Can you take me back with you to the States because Carolyn and I are having an anniversary?" I couldn't quite imagine risking crossing the border with Neal in the car, and said, "Well, we're going on to Chihuahua," whereas I would have routinely agreed, "To hell with Chihuahua, I'll drive you back to Los Gatos." But I chickened out. Have ever after been ashamed of myself for my having let a beloved friend down.

Q: How did you meet Ken Kesey?
A: Through his old wrestling coach, or English teacher, at Oregon, Philip Temko. We wrestled, Ken and I, out in front of a shack he had on Perry Lane, hard by Stanford, where he was a Stegner Fellow. Frances and I had a little bungalow on Concord Way in Burlingame and fell in with Ken through Temko and my search for Allan Temko, a writer I wanted to attract to the *Chrysalis Review*, a lit mag I was mounting at the time. So first I meet Kesey in San Jose at a romp Philip Temko was throwing. Met Neal there that night, too. Later on Kesey and I wrestled. He slaughtered me. This seemed to promote a friendship. Too, he was working on *Cuckoo's Nest*, so there was the bughouse connection. Indeed, I was incarcerated twice—for two weeks in Florida and, later, for eight months up in White Plains. I could spend forever telling you tales about Kesey and Cassady. At the time I fell all over myself in devotion to Kesey's writing. Yeah, I loved Kesey and his work. I loved the shit out of him, an utterly alive fellow, as was Cassady. But Cassady was gentle and dear and sensitive and kind. Kesey was anything but. He could be a pretty trying fellow and we became increasingly less palsy. There were all the kids he collected around his place in La Honda, that clique, and by the time Tom Wolfe turned up on the scene, I was plenty absent from it. Went up to Victoria, Canada, then to Jackson Hole, Wyoming, then on to New York. I wouldn't go along on either of the bus trips. Didn't want to surrender myself to that prankstering bit, had Frances, the children, and a job I was going, presently, not to have. Ken kept saying, "Come on, come on, come on, if you want to be my friend, come on," but I wouldn't go. Yes, we had remarkable times. He died too young. I miss him all the time. Can't say I didn't love Ken, but with Neal the affection was far less troubled. No, no trouble at all.

Q: How did you become the fiction editor of *Esquire*?
A: I was headed to New York. And Rust Hills had put the word out that he was looking for a replacement for himself. Wanted to retire. I was

recommended to him by Hal Scharlett, the editor of E.P. Dutton. So I showed up in New York and over I go to 488 Madison, to find this extraordinary figure seated in the tiny office the fiction editor occupied. The '69 World Series was playing on his radio, and he had his feet up on the desk and he seemed to me quite as glamorous as he had seemed to me from a distance and what is most memorable about the meeting was his nonchalance. He was smoking—I believe he was pretty much a chain-smoker of Camels. And he was throwing the matches into a wastebasket and had set it afire. I noticed this and with some alarm, but noticed with equal alarm that he did not seem much interested in what was beginning to be a true blaze. And I tried to catch his attention on that score and he, without even rising from his position lazing back in his chair with his feet above the desk, picked up a New York telephone book and threw it into the wastebasket and extinguished the fire. We went out the night after with Harold Hayes, *Esquire*'s editor-in-chief, and, as was the practice then, got plastered. In the course of the meal, I had the impression Hills and Hayes were not exactly sweethearts. It seems that Hills, not to mention Clay Felker and Ralph Ginzburg, all editors at *Esquire*, had been passed over for the top job when Arnold Gingrich, the publisher, awarded it to Hayes. Felker and Ginzburg quit, and Rust had stayed on in his post as fiction editor. Hayes was hardly literary in the sense that Rust was. Rust was completely charming. I don't think he expected me to last in the job. Thought he could resume his old role when he wanted it back. So, sure, there was this strain between us.

Q: Scharlett had heard of you because of the literary magazine you founded in 1962, *Genesis West*?
A: Yes, and before GW, the *Chrysalis Review* and *Why Work*. GW made far more of a mark than it deserved. In the East, they tended to romanticize everything being done in the West. Still, we brought out Kesey and Jack Gilbert and Leonard Gardner, who later denounced me, I do believe, over the Carver affair.

Q: How did you first start editing Raymond Carver?
A: I was under contract to revise *The Perrin-Smith Handbook of Current English* for Scott Foresman. My editor, Curt Johnson, came out to Palo Alto to see his people on Scott Foresman contracts, and also his contributors to his lit mag, *December*. I was both. Carver had been a contributor and, I guess, a good buddy of his. I was at Educational Development Corporation at the time, working on *A Man's Work*. So we were supposed to meet, and Johnson phoned to say, "I can't keep my appointment with you, I'm stuck

here on California Street with a guy who's too drunk to get home and his car won't start." I rode my bicycle over there. That was how I met Carver. Then it was revealed that Carver worked across the street from my office. He was a textbook editor at Science Research Associates. When I got the idea to start up a new lit mag, I thought, "Well, here's somebody who will give himself to the endeavor." On one or two occasions, he came to my apartment and I fed him lunch and we talked about starting something called *The American Journal of Fiction*. There's a photograph of Carver sitting at Barbara's and my dining table, sky-high candlesticks on it, with Ray wearing a shirt of mine. Took the picture for some book he was bringing out. By that time, Frances and I had divorced, and I was readying myself to leave town because Frances had threatened Barbara, and Barbara felt that she had nearly been run down in the street by Frances. Barbara was scared. So was I. We arrive in New York, I get the *Esquire* job, and had asked Carver if he would collect my mail for me and keep an eye on Frances and the kids—which he never, he in time confessed, did. In exchange for this, I was happy to look at his stuff. I was eager to read anybody's work who wasn't an *Esquire* regular. I read all the slush, for instance—and was less given to reacting to agented material. I wanted newcomers and was faced with the problem of satisfying Hayes and Gingrich's notion that I was going to turn up something hitherto unseen— the New Fiction. I saw in Carver's pieces something I could fuck around with. There was a prospect there, certainly. The germ of the thing, in Ray's stuff, was revealed in the catalog of his experience. It had that promise in it, something I could fool with and make something new seeming. "Fat" was the first one I revised, but Gingrich nixed it. I got it into *Harper's Bazaar*.

Carver wasn't the only one, you understand. I probably expended rather more assiduity in his case, yes. The degree of my industry was to revise a piece three, four, five times in a day. I did that on weekends, too. Not just with Ray's work. I was keeping myself alive by doctoring books as well, because the *Esquire* salary was woefully inadequate. I would get work from McGraw-Hill or Harcourt Brace—one of those outfits that was inclined to arrange a largish advance for a book they could not then publish without its enjoying a good deal of fixing. It never worked out well, however. There was always bad feeling in the end, always lunacy, particularly with ghost jobs. I can't think of very many times I did such work and it didn't end badly.

Q: Do you feel you've been demonized for your editing of Carver?
A: Indubitably. But if you look at the worksheets in the Lilly Library, they astound. No one who has not looked at the evidence could otherwise

imagine what had, in fact, occurred. For all those years. Carver could not have been more enthusiastic, nor more complicit—or complacent. That mood reversed rather sharply when he appeared at the YMHA, and I met Carver and Tess Gallagher for drinks across the street. Things between us were quite obviously going south. I took it that from that point forward she was increasingly participating in what work Ray turned out. We finished *Cathedral*, with which, it is argued, I didn't have anything to do at all, but I did, to be sure, *Cathedral* drastically less than with the first two collections—yet that was that for Ray and me.

Q: What did you have in mind when you were editing Carver's stories?
A: If I had anything in mind when I did what I did, it was James Purdy, maybe Grace Paley a little bit, but Purdy more than anyone else—stories like "Don't Call Me by My Right Name," "Why Can't They Tell You Why?," "Daddy Wolf"—writers I'd published in *New Sounds in American Fiction*, via EDC, this with Cummings, a subsidiary of Addison-Wesley. I think the heroizing of Carver is nuts. As is the defense. You take any cherished object and show, "No, no, that was made by Morty Shmulevitch on a lunch break on the line as a full-time jeweler," it's unacceptable to the fans. Nobody can quite process it, conceive of the case.

Q: If a story comes in from an unknown writer and you know you have to do so much stuff to make it worth running in a big magazine like *Esquire*, why accept it at all?
A: To produce this so-called New Fiction. One had to devise it out of what one had, and I had Carver and plenty of others from slush. Doing, as you put it, "so much" was not a difficulty for me. I probably welcomed the opening.

Q: When you gave your archive to Indiana, did you know it would set off a controversy?
A: I may have hoped so. When I was divorcing Frances, Andreas Brown offered me two thousand dollars for the paraphernalia that had accumulated in the production of the *Chrysalis Review* and *Genesis West*. It was staggering. We lost at least that much every time we put out a number. I saw the sense in saving everything that came to me. Everything. Under a typewriter at *Esquire* and at Knopf and at *The Quarterly*, I kept a carton and I'd drop everything in it, seal it up, and start another. When Barbara was diagnosed with ALS, the last neurologist to confirm the terrible news allowed as there was nothing to be done but to get money. I then sought to sell the papers,

worksheets, and the like. Did I think the Carver would prove, at some point, combustible? Did I hope it would? Would it, on so doing, confirm recognition of a kind I believed deserved? I'd be a liar if I answered otherwise.

Q: What did you think when you saw the worksheets after many years?
A: I was pleased. Delighted. Even flabbergasted. But Carver's were not the only ones I'd worked on to that extent. Not the only ones by a long shot. There were many. I've been decried for a heinous act. Was it that? Me, I think I made something enduring. For its being durable, and, in many instances, beautiful.

Q: If you don't think of yourself as a writer, how come there are books out there with your name on them?
A: Because I could get away with it and because it was persuasive to women. I think I'm an editor, a reviser. I think I'm a teacher. Not a writer. My son Atticus is a writer. I have the view that, in a word, in a breath, in a turn, the sublime can be created. I can do that in revising. As an editor, I stand by my taste and not by anybody else's. Am prepared to run riot exercising my druthers. Am also, as a writer, just as convinced of my elections. But regarding talent, nah, I have nothing of consequence, although I'm a sucker for my own work.

Q: Was it ever your ambition to approach the sublime?
A: Oh sure. But never came close. You have to have an interest in the world to capture the sublime. I'm not interested in the world. You have to have an interest in people. Apart from my relations as a father, a husband, a lover, I'm not interested in people. I'm not really terribly interested in anybody else's heart or mind, or even in my own. The great affection of my latter years, I attend to her bearing but not as I imagine others would and do. I'm not exactly autistic, but if you called me that, I wouldn't object. Hey, I've been fired from every job I've ever had. I can manage, if I choose to manage, but I don't choose to. Really, the society of others—certain friends, family, and lovers aside—is not a prominent need in me.

To bring about the kind of work that has been brought about by a person we would cite as possessed of the power to sweep us away, one would have to be interested in others, in nature, in the machinery of the given. One would have to be interested in what's without. I so often don't even notice it. If I were to walk to the grocery, I will glance at a woman on the way but walk right past a war breaking out, not thinking anything of it. I would note a datum in the margin. Not so with DeLillo, for example, his apprehension of the details of the world. Not so with Cormac McCarthy or with Sam

Lipsyte, for further example. Numerically speaking, for further example, I'm two times more of a father than Lipsyte is and six times a grandfather but could never render the fairly universal experience Lipsyte has of a father having lost sight of his child in the course of a visit to the park. Look at Lipsyte's *The Ask*—it would just be completely beyond both my ken and my reach, to do what he did with his Bernie's falling from view. It's not that I can't register it—it can be vivid for me—terrifying, of course, but I could never summon the terms of the actuality to enact the matter in prose. I'm a poseur, a potzer—not a writer in the sense that matters. Shit, are you kidding? The sublime.

Q: You brought it up, the sublime.
A: Right. But not with respect to my own writing. Only, if ever, through my acts of revising the materials of others.

Q: You approach the sublime through editing?
A: By revising, let's say, yes. Or so I prefer to claim.

Q: Do you think that's the case with Carver, or are you thinking of other writers?
A: I'm thinking of anybody whose work I've fooled around with. Had I not revised Carver, would he be paid the attention given him? Baloney!

Q: You enter into counterfactuals. The question is muddled by history.
A: Bullshit! I was there before there was a record to suffer muddling, confusion, sides taken. I can't believe that what I had in my hands from Ray would have made its way into the hearts of those who have apparently been so undone by the work. Which work had been deformed, reformed, tampered with in every respect by, yeah, me. Contaminated, uncontaminated, that's a discrete consideration. But readers were seduced, and, I'm sorry, but it was my intervention that seduced them. In it, in doing this, I fashioned a golem that would be cheered to see me destroyed. It's nothing but a botheration to me. What have I done? What have I done? I did no different, or no differently, with others' work, and some were supremely grateful for it, and not silent about their debt—Barry Hannah would be such a person. But Hannah, dear Barry, he was a mensch and a half.

Q: You were talking about your inability to apprehend the word when you walked down the street or to put your experience into words. What is the difference between that and sitting down with the text as an editor?

A: Entirely separate actions of the mind, of the heart. Words seem to me safe sites for me to inhabit. I think I've always been afraid of everything actual, and less afraid—or not afraid at all, finally—of what can constitute the made, and the made apart from the given. I'm afraid of my children. I'm afraid of my wives. I'm afraid of my friends, of my father, of you. I find succor in my playthings, the components of a composition I'm conniving with. I expect I'm just a fearful fellow, paranoid. It has lots, I'd guess, to do with my size, my skin, my sense of being Jewish. But when I read, when I edit, or revise, I don't fear anything in the least. I feel at home, at peace, assured. I feel welcomed—from what prompts I do not know. I was a boy who listened to his mother. I can recollect better my father's diction than I can my father. I was made to keep to my bed a lot—and this habitat sponsored in me much in the way of solipsism. I was never anxious when off by myself.

Q: How can you tell what's good? How can you tell shit from Shinola?
A: Because I've got the fucking gift for it. Instinct, call it. Whatever the property, in truth or in delusion, I depend upon it. Without a hitch. I would regard myself as infallibly able to make distinctions between this and that, distinctions others would either not make or would withdraw from acknowledging. I would think, How can they not see? I would sit with Harold Bloom with some regularity, hand over a book I thought highly of, say, Jack Gilbert or *Blood Meridian,* and wait for him to refuse even to look. Or if he did look, he'd not seem to see in it what I'd see. Later, when he was assembling his Western canon, he stuck in, I believe, McCarthy's *Blood Meridian* and the great *Suttree.* All of McCarthy is great, save perhaps the novel that was so widely read—*All the Pretty Horses,* and *The Orchard Keeper.*

These determinations I make, rightly or wrongly, don't come about by close study but rather by sense, in the instant, no room for a second thought. My tampering, if that's the word, with this or that is an act I undertake by reason of the same sensation. Is it intuition? Or is it an act of recognizing? I feel I know something—in the Gnostic manner, say. I cannot be talked out of it, nor, for wage's sake or to hide in the general opinion, talked into it. I don't go along—but am furious when others don't go along with me. How can they not revere what I revere? How is it that my gods are invisible to them? It's inexcusable but, of course, wretchedly expectable. Am I a zealot, a terrorist, out on my own limb? Yes, with a vengeance! Just now I'm inclined to bracket a writer, Jason Schwartz, with the best—even with the far more spectacular Atticus, who takes in the whole world, and who deeply, deeply—like DeLillo, like Ozick—cares about it. Schwartz, contrastively, cares only, I'd argue, in a minor key, underscoring jots of scarcely present objects—all of it glimpsed, say, and then, as fleetingly, let go of.

Q: Are there nameable qualities you look for, that your charismatic sense detects?
A: Difference—that's it. To say originality would be nonsense. What's original? Or, worse or better, aboriginal? Energy? That was Paley's determinant. Work, blood, the daily. I don't know, I can't say. I know it when I have it in hand. But I know it immediately. First reading DeLillo, his "In the Men's Room of the Sixteenth Century"—in a sentence I knew where I was. It is why I think Denis Donoghue exhibits, in a sentence, that no one can write an English sentence and beat him at it. Take Joy Williams's recent *New Yorker* story, "Chicken Hill." In the breath before she speaks, her genius is audible.

Q: Are you interested in anyone else's opinion?
A: No, not really, or, more truly said, not at all. Would I be persuaded by anyone else's opinion? Fat chance! Try to build a brief against Jason Schwartz, whoever you are—you'd get nowhere with me. I love for life. You could sooner divide me from Rusty or from Paco, the dogs of my heart—and I'd've *killed* for them.

Q: You say you are also authentically a teacher—indeed, you're known for your writing classes. How did that come about?
A: I taught writing at the College of San Mateo when I was teaching high school in Millbrae, California. Then, when at *Esquire*—in '71, perhaps—at Yale. The rule was you could take no more than fifteen students. I took as many as could fit in the room. Had to, after some years of commuting once a week, quit. Was nailed on a matter of political incorrectitude. They'd probably get me on darker shit now, though. I am not in the business of accommodation.

Q: Did you call the class a workshop?
A: No, I called the class a class. It went on well past the official closing time. Derrida's did, too. We'd meet, after hours, in Naples, the pizzeria. Thereafter, at Columbia, NYU, and when I set up a private group, we'd start at six and go to midnight or later. In Chicago and Bloomington, some classes went ten hours without letup.

Q: So what happens? You lecture?
A: I talk. When I run down, I keep talking. When I am done in, I ask a student to read. Then, on the evidence of the first sentence, I find the ground to resume talking.

Q: What is the format?
A: There is none. What occurs to me at the time as feasible, profitable, called for.

Q: Do you consider it a form of performance?
A: You bet. But what do we do that's not? Even when we're hysterical or frightened to death, we're deploying the vanities and falsifications of performance. What's not an act? Even in seeming solitude, do we not feel ourselves called upon to dissemble for the gods?

Q: So you just talk—no bathroom breaks and no questions?
A: No, no, there's freedom to piss if a student wants. But since I don't, most, if not all, follow suit. Or try to. Listen, I don't recommend it. Atticus says I have a boggy bladder. Please that this were my only punishment for behaving as if I could get away with beating the rap.

Oh yes, there was the exception of Noy Holland. Only once has a student read an entire composition in class, and that was Noy Holland, who read until two in the morning a longish story called "Orbit," recited it from beginning to end. There were maybe twenty-five people in the room. Nobody moved, nobody made to go. Some people in those days would come from far away. Someone would commute from California, one from Vienna, another from Paris, there were a number from Chicago who would come twice a week when I was holding the class twice weekly, a number came from far upstate New York and from Boston. None of the workshop stuff. None of it. Ever. No reading your work, everybody sitting with a photostated copy of it, everybody commenting, the teacher summing up the various pros and cons, then closing with the ex cathedra view. There was no setup like this in the class. It was about teaching, not about opining and therefore the politics that ensues from what is inexorably a social engagement, with factionalism developing, skirmishes planned. The thing has been much reviewed—and, I would imagine, reviled or, for novelizing's sake, seen as vitriol or opportunism. The actress Laura Linney's father, Romulus Linney, published a swell short story satirizing, or lampooning, a workshop of the kind. Yes, it was quite a fine piece, as I recall—with a superb conclusion.

Q: What effect does your class have?
A: I think a third leave enraged. I imagine they have come for different treatment than what they receive. I think a third continue writing as they had. And a third, I reckon, are changed. At any rate, I keep up with the fortunes of very few. Too many students, so many outcomes—some powerfully other than what one might have guessed. Many have benefited from "networking," it seems—doing very well for themselves by spreading their range of friendships and relying upon favors. They come to find out can I have your agent, can I have your publisher, can I have a tip or two or three or four. These are what are being pegged as "creative-writing professionals." But we live with others, make our lives with others. I knew Curt Johnson. Ray Carver knew Curt Johnson. We both had had work in Johnson's *December.* Then I get the *Esquire* job and Carver's writing makes its way, however altered, into *Esquire.* Is this not the course of every aspect of the human endeavor—or call it hustle? Let me tell you, I'm happy to keep in touch with my precious Patty Marx.

Q: How have you been spending your time lately?
A: I watch TV. All the channels, all the crap, back and forth. I find it a great substitute for living. I have no complaint with it. No Baudrillard bellyaching here! But don't have any other screens. I can spend forever with C-Span. Listen, you're talking to someone who, when a boy, would, for hours, sit before the test pattern quite happy with its content. One would study it for changes of the subtlest kind, probably seeing distinctions that were not there. Like someone in the loony bin listening to the wall, waiting for the wall to speak, being vexed when it doesn't, then hearing it when it isn't. Accompanying the test pattern was a hum, and eventually music. I was stirred by these presences—and made quite at peace with myself. One loves the shamelessness of channel 13 or PBS, its running a bit by Edward R. Murrow in which he announces the inauguration of public broadcast, promising the absence of commercials. Now look! Ah, promises. When Barbara could do nothing else, TV was salvation. Thank God for it. Had she lived till digital times, her suffering would have been mediated by the riot of the Internet. We cherish these distractions. Without them, death, dying, waiting for the finish would be far more severe—especially if you had refused the fables and easements guaranteed by belief.

Near his death, Mailer said something worth remarking. He was with his son John Buffalo on TV—C-Span, wasn't it? Mailer said, "What's wrong with America is this—we've lost grammar." I like to think he didn't mean it metaphorically, either. He meant it as stated. Grammar, we've lost grammar. We've lost, are losing, our language—or a language. It falls away from us in tragic fragments like a disintegrating garment. It's inevitable, of course— but for those who got used to moving in that medium, it's sad. Sure, there's always new language, languages, to learn. But at eighty-two, I don't have the muscle for learning even simplisms. There is what Lecercle called "the violence of language." Its flux is deadly for those who cannot adjust to change. Shit, I don't want to adjust. If I had the muscle to do it, I'd refuse to budge. My people came from somewhere else. It cost them to make way for a child to speak a certain form of English. I suppose I don't want to take their sacrifice lightly—don't want to dishonor their gift by going along with an idiom they'd have the ear to guess was abhorrent to the mind of God. I'm no believer, but I'm not kidding or overstating. TV, even when it's C-Span's version of it—indeed, especially when it's C-Span's version of our speech and, thus, of our thinking—is another country, one where there is the remnant of grammar, but its gown's drifted off into a gully from which there is no recovering it. That's a social good, right? But it's a personal grief, a godawful heartbreak. It's okay—everybody is watching the show!

Take basketball. It's not played as it once was. DeLillo used to insist that the way the game is now played exhibits far more skill and verve and theater. Don and I go back to the days of George Mikan and the hook shot. There's none of that anymore. Everything is always something else. As DeLillo writes somewhere, you go to bed and in the morning get up and see everything changed around. It's been rearranged, in the night, all of it. That's the deal for every living one of us. I'm certain it's beautiful, I'm certain it's ineluctable. I'm even convinced it's the expression of genius on the job. Genius! But for me, it's spooky, unbearable, incoherent, theft. Life's a war zone. Death's the sanctuary. You want to be safe? Or in unspeakable disarray? These are the bleatings of an old man who just seeks to get older and be left alone while he's trying to do it.

An Interview with Gordon Lish

David Winters / 2015

From *Critical Quarterly*, 57:4 (2015), pp. 89–104. Reprinted by permission.

David Winters: You're widely regarded as one of America's most influential teachers of creative writing. Can we begin by looking back at your early experiences of teaching and learning?
Gordon Lish: We must first accomplish some satisfactory understanding of whether writing can be taught. In my view, it can, but not to very many. A number of my students have gone on to produce commercial work; the kind of writing I don't admire. But some have emerged to take the form and manipulate it to their own liking—writers like Jason Schwartz, Sam Lipsyte, Sam Michel, and Noy Holland. There are scores more, going all the way back to Opal Belknap, the first student I taught, at a junior college in California.

When I was younger, I had taken a creative writing class myself—at the University of Arizona, where I first ran afoul of, and then developed a great affection for, a fellow named Edward Loomis. Loomis was a hard case. He affected the air of a Hemingway around campus, and had fought in the Second World War. All I really wanted to do was write. I didn't care about anything else. At the very first class, Loomis found what I had written publicly far from up to par. And I cried. I was overwhelmed with tears, and beat my way to the door and home. Years later, though, I became good buddies with Loomis. I grew deeply fond of this man, who had made me cry as a boy.

Early on, I was fired from teaching high school in California. One of my students there was J. Craig Venter, who has since come close to a Nobel Prize for his work in biology. He was in a class of students who had to have an IQ superior to a certain amount. This was a highly competitive setting, in which I fomented as much rivalry as I could—much as I later did in my writing classes. Anyway, the school refused to renew my contract. It was an extremely conservative school district, and I was cited as a danger to the students—for the silliest reasons. I would bring Ken Kesey and Neal Cassady into class. I didn't oblige the kids to get under their desks during bomb drills, and I didn't pledge allegiance to the flag. Eventually it became national news; *The Nation* covered it, and there was a trial. It wasn't the last job from which I was fired.

Q: Let's discuss the ideas behind your teaching. I'm especially interested in your thoughts on literary originality. In the past you've suggested that every human being possesses, at some buried level, a unique relation to the grammar of their native language—what you've sometimes called an '*Ur*-language.'

A: Yes. In the old days, I called it a *khora*. An innate melody that some psychoanalysts would claim issues out of the melody of our name, or whatever affectionate name we might be given by our parents. Early in life, we have established within us a certain brief musical jotting. This is what is elaborated if we spread ourselves out into acts of writing. It can be seen in the writing of others, but I believe that it can also be consciously elicited. In order to do so, you must understand that you're safest when you're at your most honest—which I would be quick to justify my own scribbling as being. In my writing, I'm psychopathically engaged with the phonemic; the smallest spicule of the construct is a concern to me. At the same time, I try to give way to a speech which has its origin somewhere well beyond my understanding. It is as if something interior is determined to speak.

This sounds preposterously operatic, but most if not all of what I've done has been in the way of releasing myself, or getting a look at myself that I otherwise would not have had. Although I'm erratic and flamboyant when I'm teaching and giving talks, in life I tend to be not a little shy and constrained. And yet, in my writing, I'm not. And by writing I find out, bit by bit, who I am and what has animated me. What we're really talking about here is the claim that one can both exert extreme control over the properties of speech, and at the same time be free. And I take the view that one can.

Q: As you know, the term *khora* crops up in Julia Kristeva. There are many references to philosophy in your work—especially in your novels, which draw from Deleuze, Adorno, and Agamben, among others. How did you develop an interest in this material?

A: A program of that kind of reading has been a habit for a long, long time. Part of it was to lend credibility to my having the cheek to teach. You tend to look everywhere for reified versions of notions you already have. I'm now reading Erving Goffman's *Frame Analysis*, since I've often posited a notion of "the frame," and of how the frame comes into being—but of course Goffman has something entirely different in mind. So, I try to revise. If I read a philosopher, and he's not interested in what I'm interested in, I'll revise what he's said, to bend it to my uses. For example, my next book has an epigraph from Agamben. I had read this passage, and written it down. And in writing it down I broke it up into lines, as if it were poetry—and I *changed* a word or two. Something I have done over the course of the years more widely than is recognized. Actually, this is the first time I've admitted to it. For instance, with one of Carver's books, I added a comment from Frank Kermode. Kermode had never made such a statement. I figured he would never see it, or that if he did, he would say, "Oh, that's Gordon, that's OK," and he would forgive it. I knew Kermode through Denis Donoghue. I would do that with some regularity. How did I get interested in philosophy? It was a rearguard action. I was hoping to give substance to that which I said. But in order to do that I would have to *revise* the philosophy. If I were reading Schopenhauer, I would have to bend it and change it, to make it come out my way.

Q: When you were teaching, which writers did you ask your students to read? Did you ever recommend works of philosophy, alongside fiction?
A: I did recommend philosophy, although I tried to focus their attention on the short story. It's preposterous to think that you can undertake a novel without having first done short stories. I was concerned to raise in people an awareness of the short story as a form, and to devise methodologies that would put that form within their reach. I wanted them to find themselves succeeding at bringing about a completion, a total effect of some kind. As praxis, you can't do that with a novel. And the kind of class I had, it was not Iowa. I would get up and scream for six to ten hours, and then hope that someone would come in the next week with something finished. I think most people went away completely bewildered. As regards philosophy, I would do what I could to legitimate my posturing by peppering my speech with the names of the august. I didn't require my students to make a study of it, but many have. Not a few have switched fields entirely. As for fiction, back then, it was people like, say, Stanley Elkin. I regard "A Poetics for Bullies" as a kind of map of how it's done. What the artist is, is Push, the bully. Grace Paley would be another person in that group. Donald Barthelme would be another.

Q: You taught creative writing at several universities. Can you share any memories of that time? When you began teaching privately, did the content of your classes change?

A: At Columbia, I remember the class went from fifteen to one-hundred-and-twenty students. I said, "I'm not keeping anybody out. Anyone who wants it can come. It won't mean more work for me, since I'm not going to read every word they write." Having been an editor, I had gotten to believe that I could merely look at the work, look at the first page, and within instants know if it required further investigation. This may be insanity in the extreme, but I had the view of myself that this was my gift. That I could see, from the configuration of the first page, whether it was worth going further.

In my private classes, I was teaching people whose investment in the undertaking was clearly more intense than at the universities. So, I felt that I had to have in my kitbag that which was available nowhere else. The brush with which I've been tarred, all the rumors, all of this issued out of those latter years. I exerted some pressure on students to retire. And many did. The class became a more difficult undertaking to endure. But those who got through, who stuck it out, were of a different kind from those that took flight. I say this fully mindful that when Loomis made me cry, I took flight. I went home to my wife and sobbed about this bully who just beat me up. And here I was, doing far, far worse. The popular methodology of the time—the "Lead, Kindly Light" approach—was inimical to my muses.

In my case, if you had a sentence, I'd want to hear you say it. And you might utter no more than four words before I'd tell you to stop. You know, the other night, I had dinner with some friends and their daughter. The daughter began a sentence with the words "I mean I think." Five minutes subsequent to that moment, her father asked me what I did in my class. And I told him this: if a student said "I mean I think," I'd say, "That's four beats you've expended. But you don't understand. You have a *life* that's four beats long. That's it. You get four beats." I'm thinking of physics; that argument between Einstein and Bohr about what happens inside the electron. The span of our life, if construed in relative terms, may be no longer than four beats. And if you say "I mean I think," you've used those four beats to say nothing. I tried to convince my students that every utterance must have substance, must occupy the instant utterly, fully.

I preferred teaching to anything else that I did. I could not have taken myself more seriously. I would try to get my students to understand that what they were doing was a matter of life and death, that the soul was involved, and that the only important things were the self and the work—certainly not newspapers or sales. So many writers today are only involved in the social act. But if you're playing the game in that way, you can't possibly play the game with art itself. If you're involved in these activities that are peripheral to the creation of art, you're not, indeed, yielding to your *khora;* you're not yielding to the truth that's in you.

Q: What do you make of the rise of the MFA program? Over the course of your career, you witnessed an enormous shift in American literary culture.
A: I did a lot of travelling, before my wife got ill, and I saw the whole university scene. I never liked what I saw. One time, sitting in on a class at the University of Texas, I just stood up and said, "I can't bear to observe this." Fiction matters to me more than anything else in the world. It matters to me more than my life does. It's like saying I'll die for being a Jew, I'll be killed for being a Jew. Or I'll be killed for having psoriasis. These particularities come closer to naming and identifying me than anything else, and my feeling about prose fiction is that it's on a par with these concerns. And here was someone coming into my synagogue, as it were, and desecrating the whole place. It was all "Who's your agent?" "Who's your publisher?" I got up in the midst of it and created a scandal. If you were my student, I would try to persuade you that you don't want to have a life where your consort is Mammon. You don't need the assent, the approval, the admiration of anyone. You are fulfilled by reason of your having placed yourself inside an infinite space that's bounded on either end, or bounded all around, in such a way as to bring a totality into effect. That should be enough.

Q: I'm fascinated by this idea of an "infinite space" that's "bounded all around." You've said some interesting things about bounded infinities before—in your lecture "Death and Language," for instance, where you explore the fractal structures inside sentences. Is the creation of such spaces the ultimate goal of writing for you?
A: That's what it is for me. I think the sentence and the work might both be defined as that: an infinite space, bounded nevertheless. And if you'll allow the contradiction, a total effect arising out of this. I know it can be done. I know it's done by Don DeLillo. I know it's done by Cormac McCarthy. It has long been my view that in the business of making sentences, these two persons cannot be improved upon, at least in the long form. They don't just deliver an impression of the object. They see the object entire. They see all its parts, and all its extensions. They see all around it. It's infinite in that sense: they see it all. They're both poets, great poets of the sentence. This is

why I resent, say, Philip Roth so entirely. I don't think he cares about sentences. Whatever he cares about—making political points, making social points—it's not literature by my lights. Not at all.

Take, by contrast, a student of mine, Jason Schwartz. I'm amazed by what Schwartz sees in the lacunae; the way he makes the lacunae brim with feeling. Writers like Roth, people say they're about big things, not nebbish stuff like Schwartz. They're not interested in a mote of dust falling on a table; they're interested in the world turning. I say they don't know shit about the world turning. But Schwartz *knows* about the mote of dust. He's seen it. That's true. That's honest. He focuses his attention on what he knows. But he'll never be celebrated, and it breaks my heart. It's a true invention; there's nothing like it around. And if he can do it, someone else can do it. Flannery O'Connor could do it: "She would have been a good woman if it had been somebody there to shoot her every minute of her life." There are people who can do it with just *one sentence*, and you'll never forget that sentence. And then there are those who can't do it with hundreds.

Q: Critics of you and your "school" have dismissed your interest in the sentence as trivial and superficial. Sven Birkerts once called it an "abrogation of literary responsibility." But my understanding is that your aesthetic contains a strong moral component.

A: Yes. This sounds screwy, but that moral component—or rather, that overlay—is a result of one's having undergone certain considerations in the course of *making* the sentence. The maker of the sentence is involved with *all* of the properties of language that exist in that sentence. And in this respect, there is no difference between the beginning and the end of the sentence. It's all of a thing, and it is infinitely elastic. You can do anything with it you want. I taught my students to orchestrate a concatenation of sentences, each issuing out of the prior one. I know that you've already written about what I call "torsion" and the "swerve"—where every sentence is in contest with what has been said. That's what it is. The moral work occurs when the writer is confronted with all of the pathways that might be illumined by reason of what he has said, and he considers them for their relative depth of engagement; their relative danger. The way in which each one promises or fails to promise to open, deepen, reveal.

Ordinarily, quite the opposite occurs. The safest pathway is chosen. That which seems most in keeping with tradition; with what is conventionally done. But I say that you must refuse and refuse and refuse. It's really Fiedler's "No! In Thunder"—it's about saying no always to what is prior. And by saying no to what is prior, you eventuate into a statement that you could not have conceivably arrived at otherwise. Whenever one follows the narrative arrow towards the next recognizable, feasible, sane stroke of discourse, one is captured, trapped in the trap of the trap of what has been said. I say, no! Contrarily, one should try to say what has *not* been said; what is sayable only by controverting what has been said. And *you're* the one who has said it, so you're controverting *yourself.* If you keep this behavior up, you are brought, it seems to me, all the way around to the beginning again. You have created a nimbus, a totality which will be possessed of differences that would not otherwise have come about. All by reason of imposing upon your progress, your "narrative," a refusal rather than an approval.

Now, in saying all this, I'm not calling for an end to the logic of discourse—but what kind of logic? It comes down to this: a new thing can only be done if it comes out of oneself, solely. Is this solipsism? How could it not be? What the hell is wrong with solipsism? What I want when I'm in the presence of a writer is that person's soul. The more solipsistic the better. People say, "Don't you want to communicate?" No, I don't want to communicate. I want communion. I want mutuality. I want to enter the being of the other. I want unimprovable illumination. I want to see the nature of things.

Q: Do you see anything like a rebellious spirit in contemporary fiction? Are today's writers capable of what Fiedler called the "Hard No," or are they merely yes-men?
A: Most of the books published now are *expectable* from word one. One knows that one will never encounter the heart of the speaker. The speaker has put his heart somewhere else, and has gotten down to the business of making as *many* people as possible pay attention to what is being said. I don't want the attention of many. I want the attention of the one or two who might be able to descry the minor differences—a "wiggle" where a "waggle" might otherwise have been. "Ah," they might say, "that's a wiggle—he wiggled there. He couldn't waggle, but he wiggled. And in electing to wiggle, he revealed the heroic heart of the champion."

If we go back to Beckett, or to various bits by Thomas Bernhard, these examples seem to represent an *exception.* One wants to find the new. And, in finding it, do everything one can to fight for it. There was a time when I was far more bellicose than I am now. I loved getting on panels and saying, "Well, piss on you all: if you haven't read a Raymond Carver story, you haven't read the best thing in short fiction." They'd say, "Raymond who? Raymond what?" Now, to be sure, I *wrote* those stories. But they dismissed

Carver. They only came around to him when he was officially approved, by the *New York Times* and so on. No-one's approving Jason Schwartz, I can assure you. And we know why. A Carver story is teachable. You can put it in front of a class of high school kids, and they'll get it. Not so with Schwartz. He presents certain problems. These arise doubtless out of his being smarter, and being concerned with telling the truth—his truth, uniquely.

Rebelliousness? If I can advert again to Craig Venter: this is someone who went on to be hated. Everyone hated him, because he was trying to patent genes—doing the devil's work. He recognized no God but himself. The same was true of James D. Watson—an old friend of mine—when he and Crick were accused of stealing others' data. In the name of science, they were not at all hesitant to transcend certain rules, a certain ethic. And the same must be true of musicians and painters. But for some reason, writing, or "literature" as we like to call it, seems defeated in this way. Now all you have is people like Franzen, wanting as many people as possible to read their work. I don't understand that ambition. I taught my students that they should want only the *right* readers. "Fame," or a "career," from my point of view, are not one wants to have as an artist. One wants a certain amount of distinguished recognition, but apart from that, one must be satisfied by the work itself.

Q: Let's return to the idea that writing involves telling one's own "unique truth." Such truths tend to be tied up with our deepest secrets and traumas. In your classes, you asked your students to make art from their most painful losses. One quote attributed to you is this: "The thing taken from you is your gift." In terms of your methodology, do you see writing as something that has a therapeutic—or, at any rate, a transformative—effect on the self?
A: I don't see how it couldn't. The act I've described can be construed in psychoanalytic terms. If you're unpacking every word you write, looking for how it's saying something other than what you think it's saying, and exploring *that* rather than what you think it intended to say, that becomes a psychoanalytic act. Every word is evaluated for where the prevarication is, or where the effort to conceal oneself is. Eventually, one should come to know oneself. And going into the darkness can bring about the best that life has to offer. This is why I think there's more truth in one sentence of my student Gary Lutz than in all of Roth. Lutz *gives himself away*. "The speaking subject gives herself away," says Julia Kristeva. I thoroughly believe that. What you see in Lutz, his lavish gift, is his *refusal* to relax his determination to uncover and uncover. It is, by my lights, quite wonderful, quite terrific.

Let me illustrate. Years ago now, Lutz visited with his second wife. They were on their honeymoon. We went to a Mexican joint nearby. And I noticed that he had his glass of Coca Cola situated in such a way that the overhead air conditioner was dripping directly into it. It was raining outside, and amid the downpour and the condensation, his Coke was filling up with the overflow from the unit. I pointed this out to him three or four times, and he *never moved the glass.* He kept drinking. I would expect that somewhere along the line, his refusal to do the sensible thing gave him the ground for a sentence, or even a story. What I'm talking about, and what I tried to teach, is a way of being a writer or an artist that *involves the whole of the life.* In the same way that might be said of Ken Kesey. Kesey was a lesser writer of course; Lutz is entirely the real thing.

Q: In 2010, O/R Books published a collected edition of your complete stories. The book I regard as your masterpiece, *Peru*, was also recently reprinted. Could you talk in detail about your fiction? Also, had you written much before your first novel, *Dear Mr. Capote?*
A: Before *Capote,* I was doing a good deal of ghost-writing. Then my agent for my ghost-writing work said, "You ought to write something sincere." I took the view that there couldn't be anything sillier than producing sincere work. Writing is after all an impersonation to begin with; it's a disguise. Then I saw in some tabloid newspaper an advertisement for a book publicizing the crimes of a serial killer, David Berkowitz. I was astounded. Instead of shame governing the case, it was renowned. That was what set me in motion. I came up with the idea of someone who's desperately in need of money, and who thinks he can manipulate himself into a position where he is confessing crimes that he would never actually undertake.

In writing that book, I had nothing buttressing my progress except what might suffice as an extension of the voice: writing in such a way as to appear insane. Originally I had written it so that it turned back on itself, in a Möbius strip. The beauty of it was this flourish at the end, where it was revealed that it was all in the mind. Which is not to say that it was "all a dream," which would be shameful. But I got a call from my agent, who said that my editor thought this unacceptable. He said that no one would understand the inversion I had produced. And I gave in. It remains the most vivid moment for me. I'm not given to capitulating. I abased myself, and now I'm too old, too tired to revise or rewrite it.

The second novel, *Peru,* was written with theory in mind. I knew exactly what I was doing. I didn't know where I was going, but I knew that I had in me a methodology by which I would not stay stuck in the same place. I knew that the way forward would be open to me if I had the whimsicality and the wistfulness and the recklessness to proceed. Although sloppily done, I thought *Peru* was true to the heart. Not at all true to experience, of course. In the book, "Gordon" murders the kid next door. In real life, I was the one hit on the head by a neighborhood kid with a toy rake, and went home, and my mother fainted when she saw me bleeding. My fiction is full of such substitutions and distortions. But I felt *Peru* was legitimate, and it brought me back to the belief that I could write.

In my subsequent books, I have tried each time to seek a different model. But the more I have tried, the more I can see I'm stuck in the same place. I cannot elude my tricks. I am governed by the limits of my repertoire. As you know, narrative is not the issue with me, but rather the means by which I "proceed." And yet, in proceeding, I find that I'm stuck. I don't have what it takes to be a novelist, and most of my so-called short stories are simply finger exercises. I don't take myself seriously as a writer. I take myself seriously as a teacher. And less so as an editor. I am probably a bad editor.

Q: In what sense?
A: Because if you put something in front of me, I must have my way with it. As a writer, I would never accept that. It would be unthinkable to me that I would let my work be worked over by an editor. And yet, over the years, I became caught up in revising others' writing exactly to my liking. I was unrelenting in my zeal to see to it that down to its last period, everything was in place as I would wish it. This practice was hardly confined to Carver. It was widespread. Carver was the one who took off; the one people talk about. In many other cases I applied the same rigor of attention. I played, it may be claimed, an unjust but at the same time gifted hand at bringing a worthiness out of the work that I published. I got into it, all right. But it's all in my archive. No use in talking about it; you'll have to see.

Q: Let's talk more about your fiction. I've always been struck by that statement at the start of *Capote*: "The reason is to try out voices." Where does your writing's distinctive "voice" come from?
A: It comes right out of my mother and father. I find that yielding to the speech practices of my mother and father frees me in a way I otherwise don't feel free. Even if it means drowning myself in cliché, as I did in *Capote*. Perhaps it's because they're both dead. But I get some sense of being *connected* with them; connected with their oddness in the world, their

wrongness in the world. I wouldn't try to write like anybody else. I don't write like DeLillo or McCarthy. I don't write like Grace Paley. I couldn't if I tried, but I wouldn't try.

My aim is to individuate myself as much as I possibly can. Even at the cost of appearing clownish. In my last book I took to repeating instances of my name, like so: "Gordon (Gordon!)" Which amuses me hugely, and takes on, after a time, a certain kind of life. It is a kind of "gaming," in Lyotard's sense. I'm amused by it, and I would want my reader to be amused by it. So much of what I do comes about in this way, through revisions of revisions of revisions, and by pointing out choices that might have been made. Most of my short stuff is just a way of saying, "This could not be written." It's as if I'm in the grip of a move I made on the dance floor, when I put my foot this way rather than that way. And now I'll be damned if I'm going to withdraw my foot. I'm going to keep going.

Q: I'd been searching for metaphors to describe your approach to narrative form; this one seems to capture it quite closely. Would you say that you taught the same sort of "dance moves" to your students? Did you also apply them to your work as an editor?
A: When I was stable on my feet, I used to show my students how to move backwards. First you would plant your foot on the floor in such a way that there was tension in your stance. Then you would put the toe of the other shoe against the heel of the shoe that was down—but doing so at an angle. And you would keep turning this way, backwards, until you had completed a circle. This would be the way you brought about a total effect. You don't know where you're going, you're just following your footsteps, but you're doing it backwards. You have in mind only what you've already said, and what you've already said must bring about what you are going to say. Finally, you find that you've described a circle. That's what I mean by the "frame"— a boundary that comes about through consecution. Going beyond that boundary threatens the success of the piece.

As an editor, this was the problem I had with Loomis's story, "A Kansas Girl." I included this story—which I loved, and which always made me weepy, towards the end—in a book I published called *New Sounds in American Fiction*. Later, when I was working at *Esquire*, I wanted to reprint it. I wanted to give a gift to my teacher. But when I looked at his story with the eye of an editor rather than that of a reader, I realized I'd have to *fix* it. I'd have to eliminate all of it to get from the first to the last paragraph, which was so beautiful. The problem was that Loomis wasn't able to contain the thing in that given space. He had to keep going outside of it, usually for information's sake. Usually for what amounts to a kind of flashback, which is almost always the platform on which information is delivered. From my point of view, information is anathema to feeling. The more information you give the reader, the less feeling you will generate.

Q: You've outlined an approach to literary composition which pits each sentence, each statement, against its precursor. But conflict and combat have been central to your career, not just your philosophy.
A: One is always involved combatively. As a small person, I'm inclined to see my life as combat after combat. The life that I enjoyed in the *Esquire* job or at *Genesis West* or Knopf or *The Quarterly* was all about being provocative, and waiting for him who would reply to my provocation with an illumined thought on the matter. Now that I'm old, that's what I miss the most. Back then, there was a sense not only that literature was taken seriously, but that it merited elevation to a duel. There was more of what we called *push-back*. That doesn't go on anymore; no one takes sides. The fog-machine has done its work in all the corners of the world, and there's no fight left in anyone.

So, something has changed. Of course, book publishing was already changing when I worked at Knopf. When Robert Gottlieb was running Knopf, he didn't care if I only sold one hundred copies of this or that. I would go to him and say, "I think this will do rather well in the marketplace," and he would say, "It's not for you to think about that. I just want you to find stuff that nobody else can find." That wasn't the view when Sonny Mehta took control, and it isn't at all the view in publishing today. On the other hand, here and there, small publishing houses seem to be paying attention to people that I would pay attention to. One hopes that your generation might invert the whole thing; that the pendulum might swing the other way. They'll look at all these books that are published and realize they can't sustain it. They're all copies, all fakes. At some point it all has to implode. And it may be the small presses, or the Internet, that bring that about. I'm dubious, but willing to hope.

Q: Looking back on your life, how do you feel about the reputation you've acquired?
A: As you know, the general take on me has always been, "Oh, he's out of his mind. He's dangerous socially. He's not to be taken seriously by any means. He's profited greatly on the naiveté of hundreds of young people." And I'm certain that will be the concluding take on me. But it doesn't matter. I've

never beseeched the approval of the group. To take the matter at hand seriously, one has to do a lot of avoiding. I used to encourage my students to purify the gaze, purge it of gossip and spite. My . . . in Yiddish it's *nachas*; my joy comes from making the thing. Maybe everything I say issues out of bitterness. But I've been asked, more than once, "If they offered you the Nobel Prize, would you take it?" No. I don't want their approval. That's not what I'm after. The extent to which I'm excluded is the extent to which I feel I've succeeded. The only thing that troubles me greatly is that persons who have notably studied with me would be ignored or misunderstood in the same way.

Q: And how do you feel about the future?
A: Oh, I'm too old. When my wife Barbara, who died over the course of eight years, completed that enterprise—I was too old by then. I was eviscerated by the experience. I didn't think I could live through it, and now that I've lived through it and tried to make a life for myself thereafter, that life lacks seriousness. I'm no longer worthy to wear the clean raiment; I've been stained too much by the experience of caring for her, and of her dying. And of seeing in myself my selfishness and ruthlessness. The base from which one would speak with authority has been eroded by reason of self-interest, of guardedness. I think that might be said.

David, I don't know whether I've given you anything of great profit. One shoots one's mouth off *ad libidum,* and later looks back, and is astonished at how one has gotten it wrong. Look, one knows this, and perhaps it is not as widely known as it once was: there is a celestial choir that has sung uniquely and memorably and for the profit of all mankind. And that choir is not accumulating itself now in the way that it once did. One has to begin from the position that there is greatness; that there is great writing. Beckett's *Endgame* is great. And if such greatness exists, how can you embark on an enterprise that would have as its endpoint anything less? Writers can accumulate riches, fame, recognition, and attention, but in doing so, they are not deriving from life the true genius of being alive.

I can open up McCarthy, I can open up any page of *Suttree,* and say, "That's magic." I want people who can make magic. That's what the job at hand is. To take the elements of the language, to take these tarnished and exhausted entities, and to cause them to *move* in a way they've never moved otherwise. To imbue them with movement through the particular imposition of one's will, one's desire. To say, "Can I make it do that? Can I make it do *that?*" When I'm reading, I want to be swept away; I want to feel that I have seen what I would otherwise never have seen. I want to be made to say, "I must change my life." The *New Yorker* recently ran a really vicious piece about my classes, distorting my idea of "seduction." Needless to say, I wasn't talking about sex. What I meant was that art should lead people away from being-in-the-world by conventional means.

Really, I'm asking that people tell the truth. It's as simple as that. Tell the truth. Tell it, knowing that no matter how hard you try, you're still not telling it truly. The very act, the very elapsing of time between the concept and the utterance already allows one to shield or protect oneself. Musicians, painters, sculptors and the like are given much more room to tell the truth; to give themselves away. In writing, one has to struggle. One wants recklessness, not reason. When I was teaching, I tried to eliminate the fear that situates itself between the writer and the word. The fear that makes writers behave as they do every day among people—that fear is useless, useless. One wants something else: a sublime cohabitation. An act of communion. That's what I think it is. That's what I'm asking for. It is the great event in human interaction; the great event in people being with people. What I want is that moment, in reading a writer, when I feel like we agree about what it means to be human. That feeling, that fleeting instant of mutuality, when we're able to say, "Oh, we got it. We got it together."

Index

Abrams, Billy, 82
Addison-Wesley, 145
Adorno, Theodor, 98, 154
Agamben, Giorgio, 68, 74, 154–55
Age of Wire and String, The, 99
Airships, 81
Aldridge, John, xi
Alfred A. Knopf, ix–x, 18, 20, 22, 24, 35, 40, 42, 43, 60–62, 67, 96, 99, 105, 137, 145, 164
Allen, Jennifer, 11
All the Pretty Horses, 148
Altmann's Tongue, 98
American Journal of Fiction, 144
Andreou, George, 115
Arcade, or, How to Write a Novel, 78, 138
Arizona, 17, 123
As I Lay Dying, 93
Ask, The, 147
Association of Literary Magazines of America, 8–9

Barthelme, Donald, 155
Baudrillard, Jean, 151
Beckett, Samuel, ix, 58, 90, 97, 159, 165
Behavioral Research Laboratories, 39
Belknap, Opal, 153
Bellow, Saul, 50–51, 94
Berkowitz, David, 161
Bernhard, Thomas, 102–3, 159
Bernie, Ben, 82

Bible, 29–30
Bigger Than Life, 140
Birkerts, Sven, 158
Blood Meridian, 51, 69–73, 77, 86, 98, 103, 148
"Bloodshed," 98
Bloom, Harold, x, 16, 29–30, 32, 34, 47, 55, 58, 62, 68, 74, 90, 96, 98–99, 103, 105, 148
Bohr, Niels, 156
"Book of Tubes," 99
Book Show, The, 60
Borges, Jorge Luis, 19, 58
"Boys on Their Bikes, The," 98
Broadcasting Magazine, 139
Brodkey, Harold, ix, 16, 19, 23, 53, 58, 69–71, 81, 90, 96, 98–99, 103–5, 137
Brother Antoninus, 122
Brown, Andreas, 141, 145
Buckley, Bill, 138
Buffalo, John, 151
Buñuel, Luis, 131
Burroughs, William S., 141

California, ix, 33, 36–39, 63, 122–23, 139, 141, 153
Camera Work, 104–5
Capote, Truman, 23, 94, 162
Captain Fiction, x, 19, 22, 60, 126, 130
Carleton Miscellany, The, 9
Carruth, Hayden, 121–22
Carson, Anne, ix, 99

Carver, Raymond, ix, 23, 60, 105, 126, 137, 143–47, 150, 155, 159–60, 162
Cassady, Carolyn, 141–42
Cassady, Neal, ix, xii, 37, 81, 90, 92, 123–24, 141–42, 154
Cathedral, 145
"Ceil," 98, 104
"Chicken Hill," 149
Chinese, 78–79, 87–88
Christianity, 33
Chrysalis Review, 142–43, 145
"Clean, Well-Lighted Place, A," 19
Coe, Christopher, 11
Cohen, Arthur, 65–66
Coleridge, Samuel Taylor, 50
collaboration, 88, 137
Collected Stories, 137
College of San Mateo, 149
Columbia University, 11, 43, 46, 67, 138, 149, 156
Coming Out of the Ice, 138–39
community, 15, 29
competition, 56, 72
Congregation, 29–30
consecution, 163
control, xi, 50, 91–93, 154
cortisone, 140
creative writing, ix, 4, 6–7, 45, 57, 153, 156
Crick, Francis, 55, 160
Cuddihy, John Murray, 31
Cummings Publishing Company, 145

"Daddy Wolf," 145
Dad Says He Saw You at the Mall, 99
Dallas, TX, 123
Davis, Jodi, 105
"Dead, The," 19
Deane, Seamus, 74
Dear Mr. Capote, 18, 22, 35, 43, 60, 67, 76, 79, 81–82, 88–89, 91–93, 137, 161
death, 41, 70, 96–97, 100, 117–18, 138, 151–52

December, 143, 150
Degas, Edgar, 43, 45
Deleuze, Gilles, 68, 98, 154
DeLillo, Don, ix, xi, 16, 19, 23, 47, 50, 58, 64, 69–71, 77–78, 81, 89–90, 98, 103, 105, 114, 136, 137, 146, 148–49, 152, 157, 163
Delirium, 114
Derrida, Jacques, 149
Dickinson, Emily, 58
Donoghue, Denis, 16, 23, 32, 47, 62–63, 68, 74, 81, 98–99, 103, 149, 155
"Don't Call Me by My Right Name," 145
Dove, Rita, 62
dreams, 128–29, 161
Dutton, E. P., 143

Educational Development Corporation, 143, 145
Einstein, Albert, 31, 55, 84, 156
Elkin, Stanley, ix, 37, 155
Emerson, Ralph Waldo, x, 32, 58
Endgame, 165
enemies, 24, 58, 99–100, 132, 135
Eno, Will, ix, 126
Epicurus, 108
Epigraph, 67–68, 75, 77–80, 89, 91–94, 106, 117, 125
Esquire, ix–x, 20, 22, 38–39, 41, 60–61, 67, 105, 126, 137, 142–45, 149, 163–64
Evenson, Brian, 98, 105
Extravaganza, 14–15, 22, 30, 60, 95, 101, 126, 132–33

Farmingdale, 112
"Fat," 144
Faulkner, William, 19, 93
fear, 15, 24, 36, 38, 45, 81, 83, 85, 97, 106, 148, 166
Felker, Clay, 38, 143
Ferlinghetti, Lawrence, 122
Ferrell, Anderson, 11, 56

INDEX

Fiedler, Leslie, x, 158–59
Florida, 87, 116–17, 142
Fokes, Frances, 4, 8, 18, 123, 138, 140–41, 144–45, 148, 156
Four Walls Eight Windows, 67, 71, 78
Frame Analysis, 155
frames, 13, 82, 155, 163
Franzen, Jonathan, 160
Freud, Sigmund, 31, 32, 55
Frost, Robert, 97

Gallagher, Tess, 145
Gardner, Jack, 143
"Gasserpod, Gasserpod," 9–10, 38
Genesis West, ix, 3–4, 6–8, 37, 39, 143, 145, 164
German Picturesque, A, 99
Gilbert, Jack, ix, 6–8, 62, 122–23, 143, 148
Gilbert, Sister Mary, 122
Gingrich, Arnold, 143–44
Ginsberg, Allen, 122, 141
Ginzburg, Ralph, 143
Goffman, Erving, 155
Goodman, Nelson, 98
Gotham Book Mart, 141
Gottlieb, Robert, 69, 164
Guattari, Pierre-Félix, 68, 98
Gutter Press, The, 62

Hannah, Barry, ix, 23, 60, 81, 137, 147
Harcourt Brace, 138–39, 144
Harper's Bazaar, 63, 144
Harvey, Giles, 137
Hawking, Stephen, 45, 48, 55
Hayes, Harold, 38, 143–44
Hegel, Georg Wilhelm Friedrich, 98
Hemingway, Ernest, 23, 153
Hempel, Amy, ix, 11, 23, 36, 60, 126
Herman, Victor, 138–39
Hewlett, NY, 138
Hills, Rust, 39, 142–43

"His Son, in His Arms, in Light, Aloft," 98, 104
Hiyate, Sam, 62
Hogan, Wayne, 99
Holland, Noy, 105, 150, 153
Hollywood, CA, 24
Holmes, John Clellon, 141
Howland, Bette, 30
"How to Write a Novel," 83
Hudson, 9
Hunter College, 31

I Look Divine, 11
Indiana University Bloomington, 137, 145
Internet, 151, 164
Interview Magazine, 96
"In the Men's Room of the Sixteenth Century," 149
"In the Year of Long Division," 98

Jabès, Edmond, 106
James, Henry, 118
Jewish identity, x, 17, 27–34, 84, 86, 129, 139, 148, 157
Johnny Johnston's Charcoal Room, 140
Johnson, Curt, 143–44, 150
Johnson, Denis, 81
Joyce, James, 22, 58

Kachel, Elsie, 76, 84
Kafka, Franz, x, 30, 32, 101, 106
"Kansas Girl, A," 58, 163–64
Kaufman, Andy, 126
Kelly, Pat, 139
Kennedy, Nigel, 61
Kermode, Frank, 155
Kerouac, Jack, 141
Kesey, Ken, ix, xii, 7, 23, 37, 109, 123–24, 141–43, 154, 161
khora, 154, 157
Kimball, Michael, 105

King, Stephen, 137
Kirkus, 18
Knopf. *See* Alfred A. Knopf
Kristeva, Julia, 47, 62, 68, 74, 76, 98, 103, 154, 160
Kundera, Milan, 23

Ladd, Alan, 84
Lamarr, Hedy, 117
Langer, Susanne, 98
language, 13, 19, 39, 46, 49, 53, 66, 68–70, 83–85, 102, 122, 152, 154, 158, 165
"Largely an Oral History of My Mother," 69, 98, 104
Lecercle, Jean-Jacques, 152
Lemann, Nancy, 23
Lentricchia, Frank, 98, 103, 105
Levinas, Emmanuel, 98, 135
Life and Times of Captain N, The, 60
Lilly Library, 137, 144
Lingis, Alphonso, 108–9
Linney, Laura, 150
Linney, Romulus, 150
Lipsyte, Sam, ix, 138, 146–47, 153
Lish, Barbara Works, 23, 24, 33–34, 58, 61, 79–80, 91, 99, 105–6, 110–11, 138, 141–42, 144–45, 148, 151, 157, 165
Lish, Gordon: Aunt Adele, 121–22; children, 33–34, 38, 58, 82, 124, 134, 140, 144, 146, 148, 150; editors and editing, 8–9, 24, 27, 29, 35, 40, 55–56, 60, 65, 67–69, 76–77, 81–83, 87–88, 93, 104, 106, 136, 138–39, 146–48, 156, 162–63; father, 27–28, 63, 73–75, 100, 110, 116, 121, 127, 132, 139–40, 148, 162–63; ghostwriting, 134, 138–39, 144, 161; hospitalization, 80–81, 121, 130, 140, 142; jail, 80–81; mother, 27–28, 73–74, 100, 107–9, 115–18, 121, 148, 162–63; radio, 17–18, 29, 39, 43, 84, 138–40; sister, 109–10, 140; stature, 73, 81, 83–86, 108–10, 148, 164; teaching, xi–xii, 4, 7, 11–13, 16, 19–20, 22, 26, 35–42, 43–46, 50–51, 53–59, 60, 63, 66, 67–68, 87, 104, 106, 128, 134–35, 137–38, 146, 149–50, 153–56, 162, 166; writing, 11–16, 27, 37, 40, 44–45, 63, 68, 70–71, 83, 106, 126, 138, 146, 149, 153, 160, 162, 165–66
literary magazines, ix, 3–4, 8–9, 15, 22, 39, 43, 56, 60, 121, 143
Livingston, NY, 140
Loomis, Edward, 37, 57–58, 153, 156, 163–64
Louis, Joe, 84
love, 35–36, 93, 116, 118–19, 123, 132–33, 142, 146, 149
Love-Lies-Bleeding, 136
Lutz, Gary, 99, 105, 126, 138, 160–61
Lyotard, Jean-François, 163

Maddow, Ben, 9
Mailer, Norman, 23, 82, 151–52
Man's Work, A, 39, 141, 143
Mao II, 70
Marcus, Ben, ix, 53, 99, 138
Márquez, Gabriel García, 23
Marx, Karl, 31, 55
Marx, Patty, 151
Mason, Jackie, 22
Mason, James, 140
Matisse, Henri, 105
McCarthy, Cormac, 51, 58, 69–72, 77, 81, 90, 98, 103, 136, 146, 148, 157, 163, 165
McEvoy, Miss, 84
McGraw-Hill, 141, 144
McGurl, Mark, ix–x
Mehta, Sonny, 164
Melville, Herman, 19
Mexico, 141
Michel, Sam, 98, 105, 153
Mikan, George, 152
Millbrae, CA, 149
minimalism, ix, 20

Moby Dick, 72
money, 3, 5, 7, 19, 24, 38, 41, 93, 123, 141, 145–46, 161
Mourner at the Door, 14, 18, 19, 21
Murphy, 90
Murphy, Yannick, 11–12
Murrow, Edward R., 151
My Romance, 60, 74–75, 102, 105
Mysterium, 111–15, 135
mystery, xi, 52, 60, 65–66

Nation, The, 63, 154
NBC, 139–40
Nesbitt, Lynn, 82
New Fiction, 22, 144–45
New Haven, CT, 140
New Sounds in American Fiction, 145, 163
New York, x, 5, 8, 15, 17–18, 35, 37, 39, 43, 61, 63, 67, 85, 99, 122, 138–40, 142–43
New Yorker, The, 69, 140, 149, 166
New York Review of Books, 98, 137
New York Times, 98, 160
New York Times Book Review, 137
New York University, 11, 43, 46, 149
Nietzsche, Friedrich, 91
Nightwork, 99
Nobel Prize, 153, 165
"No! In Thunder," 158

objects, 13, 28, 30–31, 48, 51–53, 62, 64, 79–81, 90, 95, 97, 101, 108, 116, 145, 149, 157
O'Connor, Flannery, 158
Office of Economic Opportunity, 39
O'Keefe, Georgia, 105
One Flew Over the Cuckoo's Nest, 124, 142
"On the Air," 84
"Orbit," 150
O/R Books, 161
Orchard Keeper, The, 148
Ordeal of Civility, The, 31

Outer Dark, 70, 98
Ozick, Cynthia, ix, 16, 19, 23, 30–31, 34, 47, 58, 69–70, 81, 89–90, 95, 98, 103, 105, 148

Paley, Grace, ix, 37, 145, 149, 155, 163
Pampa, TX, 17, 18, 138–39
Pantheon, 60, 62
Paris Review, xi
Partisan Review, 9, 38, 121
Party of Animals, A, 69
Pejovich, Ted, 11
Perkins, Maxwell, 137
Perrin-Smith Handbook of Current English, The, 143
Peru, 18, 22, 35, 67, 74, 84, 92–93, 137, 161–62
Perugia, Italy, 122
Phillips Academy Andover, 138–39
philosophy, 33, 68, 154–55
Picasso, Pablo, 43, 45, 105
Plainwater, 99
Playboy, 118
Poe, Edgar Allan, 58
"Poetics for Bullies, A," 155
poets and poetry, 5–9, 55, 62, 75–76, 104, 121–23, 155, 157
Powers of Horror, 68
psoriasis, 6, 17, 18, 116–17, 138, 140–41, 157
Publishers Weekly, 18
publishing, ix–x, 20, 25, 81, 105–6, 126, 164
Purdy, James, ix, 37, 145

Quarterly, The, ix, 15, 24, 35, 40, 43, 56, 60, 62, 67, 99, 105, 126, 137, 145, 164

Raffel, Dawn, 50, 53, 98, 105
Random House, x, 15, 61, 62
Ratner's Star, 114
Reading in the Dark, 74
recursion, 46

Redel, Victoria, 53, 98, 105
revision, x-xii, 30, 67, 71–72, 75–79, 83, 88–89, 92–95, 106, 115, 124, 137, 146–48, 155, 161–63
Richard, Mark, 11–12
Road, The, 136
Robison, Mary, ix
Rosencrantz Foundation, 62
Roth, Philip, 84, 158, 160

Salinger, J. D., 22, 126, 132, 141
San Francisco, CA, 17, 85, 122–23, 126, 132
Santayana, George, 120
Scharlett, Hal, 143
Schutt, Christine, 53, 99, 105, 138
Schwartz, Jason, 99, 105, 148–49, 153, 158, 160
Science Research Associates, 144
Scott Foresman, 143
Scroggins, Daryl, 25
Self-Imitation of Myself, 78–79
Shawn, Bill, 69
Shepherd, Jean, 140
Sigworth, Oliver, 135
"S. L.," 69, 98, 104
Smith College, 123
Socrates, 120, 138
Sparling, Ken, 99
Spencer, James, 8
Spiotta, Dana, 105
State University of New York, 43
Steloff, Frances, 141
Stevens, Wallace, 75, 84, 102
Stieglitz, Alfred, 104–5
Stories in an Almost Classical Mode, 53, 104
Stories in the Worst Way, 99
Strangers to Ourselves, 68
Stupefaction, The, 99
Sullivan, Maurice W., 39
Sullivan Associates, 39

Suttree, 148, 165
swerve, x, 46–47, 158
Swinburne, Richard, 70
symbols, 28–29, 51

Temko, Philip, 142
Ten Bits, 43
Tester, William, 11
Testimony, 30
Thousand Plateaus, A, 68
torque, 46–47
torsion, 158
"Traitor, The," 18
truth, 12–13, 18, 25, 51, 119, 127–28, 132, 157, 160, 166
Tuck, Lily, ix
Tucson, AZ, 86, 138, 140–41

Ulysses, 58
Under the Light, 98
Underworld, 70, 77, 89–90
University of Arizona, 57, 138, 153
University of Chicago, 33
University of Texas, 157
"Usurpation: Other People's Stories," 98

Venter, J. Craig, 153, 160
"Verona: A Young Woman Speaks," 98, 104
Village Voice, 98
Vintage, 62
violence, 86, 131

Walker, George, 141
Walter Pater, 99
Watson, James D., 55, 90, 105, 160
Wellesley College, 140
What I Know So Far, 35, 83
Where She Was, 56
Where the Road Bottoms Out, 98
White Plains, NY, 140, 142
Whitman, Walt, 58

Whittemore, Reed, 9
"Why Can't They Tell You Why?," 145
Why Work, 39, 143
Williams, Diane, ix, 99, 105
Williams, Joy, ix, 137, 149
Wolfe, Tom, 142

Yale University, 11, 43, 46, 67, 138, 149

Zimzum, 43, 60, 64–65, 68, 102, 105, 124, 137